When Rex Met Zulu

AND OTHER CHRONICLES OF THE NEW ORLEANS EXPERIENCE

T0015459

When Rex Met Zulu

AND OTHER CHRONICLES OF THE NEW ORLEANS EXPERIENCE

ERROL LABORDE

Illustrated by Arthur Nead

PELICAN PUBLISHING
New Orleans

ISBN 9781455627882

Printed in the United States of America
Published by Pelican Publishing
New Orleans, LA
www.pelicanpub.com

To Peggy Scott Laborde, who never ceases to love

CONTENTS

WAR

FINAL WORD: GESUNDHEIT!

ACKNOWLEDGMENTS

Benjamin Disraeli, the British Prime Minister (1868 and 1874-80), once said, "I feel a very unusual sensation—if it is not indigestion, I think it must be gratitude."

Never until this moment have I felt a common bond with Disraeli. However, even with a bottle of Rolaids handy, I can attest that what I am feeling is definitely not indigestion—but gratitude.

At the top of the list is my wife Peggy Scott Laborde, who is not only an Emmy-award-winning television producer and talent for New Orleans' public TV station, WYES, but she has also mastered the sometimes tedious, always laborious, yet often fulfilling process of doing the technical work to prepare an emerging book for presentation to the publisher. Besides serving in effect as the book's production manager, Peg also thankfully continued her vital role as wife and, as such, provided the support and encouragement for the project. For that, I am especially thankful.

There could be no book without a publisher and for that I am grateful that this publication carries the prestigious label of Pelican Publishing (now a part of Mount Pleasant, South Carolina-based Arcadia Publishing). Making that possible are two veterans of New Orleans publishing, Scott Campbell, publisher, and editor-in-chief, Nina Kooij. Thanks to both of them for saying, "Yes."

A very special thanks to Todd Matherne, the CEO of Renaissance Publishing. The content of this book consists largely of my "Streetcar" columns, which have appeared mostly in *New Orleans* magazine since 1989 and under the Renaissance name since 2006, as well as my weekly blogs which have been published on the company's website (Myneworleans.com) since 2007. Todd took over the company in the wake of Hurricane Katrina. Through his tilling, the company has become a garden in which editorial content has been able to grow and flourish.

During the Renaissance era, three editorial staff editors have, at different times, overseen, proofed, and commented on the content. Thanks to Morgan Packard, Ashley McLellan, and Kelly Massicot for their guidance and oversight.

"Streetcar" began in 1981 as a weekly column in *Gambit,* one of what were commonly called, "alternative newspapers." During that time, and into the present, the column has been given visual life by supreme illustrator Arthur Nead. His drawings have beautifully captured scenes of the city and its people. Read the essays and enjoy the art. My greatest fear is that posterity will argue that the book does not need all that writing, it is the pictures that count. I might one day reluctantly agree. For now, thanks to all the above for helping to give the writing a chance.

WHY? AN INTRODUCTION

New Orleans is a city that is rich with rituals, but none are as socially significant as the one that happens on Lundi Gras, the day before Mardi Gras when Rex meets Zulu. Carnival is a multi-cultural celebration in a multi-cultural town to which the founders arrived by way of the Mississippi River, one of the world's great waterways. Fittingly, the two kings meet on a stage alongside that river. As the crowd cheers and the pyrotechnics color the sky, the monarchs boogie to Carnival music in the city that invented jazz. And there is peace through revelry.

This book is a compilation of essays with the common denominators being *New Orleans Magazine* or its website, Myneworleans.com. Most of the essays were adapted from my monthly column, "Streetcar"; or from my weekly blog, *From the Editor's Room,* which is sort of like a column, but one that travels on the virtual highway.

"Streetcar" has been with me most of my career. I started working with *New Orleans Magazine* in 1989. Prior to that, I was the editor of *Gambit,* a weekly newspaper, there too writing the column, only then as a weekly. This column originated to add a touch of New Orleans color to a Baton Rouge based "alternative" newspaper called *Gris-Gris* (1973-1979). Originally, it was written by a talented local-color writer named Don Lee Keith. I admired Keith's writing very much, so I was flattered when, sometime in the late '70s, Keith had to give up the column and it was offered to me. Eventually, "Streetcar" and I would move on to the fledgling New Orleans-based *Gambit* newspaper.

Warning: Here comes one of my favorite stories: One day I was at *Gambit's* French Quarter office suffering from writer's block and trying to develop a topic, so I went for a walk along the old streets hoping to find an idea. Then, there was a sudden blast of a car horn from a vehicle shrieking to a stop. From within came a voice yelling, "Keep looking Errol, you will find it." I looked around and it was Don Lee Keith, who waved and then drove off.

He had written many columns in his day. I realized as he sped away that he knew exactly what I was doing. The moment was a bonding between the two authors of "Streetcar."

Not that I am bragging or anything, but through the years "Streetcar" has won serval first place awards from the Press Club of New Orleans in the column category. In 2013, "Streetcar" got national recognition by winning a Gold Award from the City and Regional Magazine Association, the trade organization of city magazines.

My blog began with the internet, making its debut in May 2007. To date it has won five first place awards in the Press Club's blog category.

In 1988, I published a collection of my "Streetcar" columns playfully entitled, *I Never Danced With an Eggplant (On a Streetcar Before).* The book was eventually republished by Pelican Publishing Company. A second book of the same kind, *The Buzzard Wore a Tutu,* was published in 1994. It was a good book, although one with a sad ending. Several of the shipment boxes were ruined by flooding due to Hurricane Alberto. Another story for another day.

Local-color columns of this sort are the side stories of the news. They play an important role, adding personality and anecdotes to everyday life. There are lots of stories out there waiting to be told; some best recognized through the eyes of columnists in pursuit of them. As Don Lee Keith would have advised, keep looking and you might find it.

When Rex Met Zulu

AND OTHER CHRONICLES OF THE NEW ORLEANS EXPERIENCE

BUT FIRST . . .

In 2013, Streetcar, the column I have written for New Orleans Magazine, won first place in the column category at the Atlanta convention of the City and Regional Magazine Association (CRMA). I was thrilled. This was the big one. Previously the column had been blessed to win in the Press Club of New Orleans' competition. CRMA, however, gave a chance to be judged at the national level. Column category competitions usually require submitting three articles. While I hope the judges enjoyed them all, I have a favorite. It is called "Maria at the Ballpark" and it tells the true story about the interactions with a young fan during a game of New Orleans' minor league baseball team, the Zephyrs. If this book was a baseball game, I would have chosen Maria to be the leadoff batter. . . .

Note: As an established Saints fan, there was a special satisfaction from having won a game in Atlanta.

Maria at the Ballpark

Somewhere around the sixth inning, Maria came into our consciousness. New Orleans' team (formerly known as the Zephyrs—the franchise has since relocated to Wichita where it is known as the Wind Surge) was already ahead 8-0 over the Oklahoma City RedHawks, but that didn't matter much to Maria, who had other things on her mind in addition to her ancestral preference for Hispanic ballplayers. Her parents and siblings had gone on a popcorn run. Maria stayed near her seat because she was preoccupied with her mission.

From seemingly out of nowhere, Maria, who was probably eight years old, tapped our shoulders and asked a question that has confounded philosophers for centuries. "Why," she asked with disgust, "is it always the boys that get the baseballs?" Several times that night a foul ball had bounced nearby, or a player on the way back to the dugout had flipped a ball toward the seats, but each time boys honed in—leaving Maria out.

We tried to explain that maybe boys were more aggressive at such things. "Would you fight for one?" I asked, "Yes!" she answered emphatically. Maria, who only minutes earlier had been a stranger to us, persisted: "I really, really want a ball," she kept on saying. "If you get one, please give it to me."

"Why do you want a ball?" I asked. "For my collection," she answered. I assured her I would do my best, but the truth was my chances were probably worse than hers. All my life I have wanted to catch a ball at a ballpark too and have never come close. Not only that, but I was also striking out with the night's other giveaways. We were sitting near the first base dugout, so it would have been easy to see us early in the game when Zephyr staffers stood on top of the dugout to toss t-shirts. I did not even earn eye contact. Later in the game Boudreaux, the mascot nutria, stood on the same platform and avoided us when he tossed out pizzas. Once, between innings, Boudreaux walked on the dugout waving to the crowd. I couldn't even get a high-five from him.

It must have been the seventh inning when Maria's parents returned. Shortly after I heard the girl shrieking. She was ecstatic. "I have a ball!" she shouted, "I have a ball!" "Where did you get it?" I asked. "My mom." Excitedly Maria tried to put together a supposition on how her mom got the ball. "It bounced and she reached over and caught it," Maria explained. Since I had not seen a ball land in our area recently, I asked her dad who paused and then said, rather timidly, that the mother had found it beneath the seats. That, to me, seemed rather miraculous, knowing how eagerly those dastardly boys hustle for the balls. Nevertheless, I chose to accept that answer, which sounded more magical than Mom perhaps buying the spotless ball in the gift shop during her popcorn quest. Whatever the method of acquisition, Maria was thrilled and even let me hold the sphere for a few well-guarded seconds. (Instinctively I sniffed the ball, which had that unmistakable leather and varnish smell that took me back to Maria's age when a hardball was the center of a boy's summer pastime, before it became a metaphor for life.)

For the Zephyrs it had been a big night. They won 11-1, not giving up that last run until the ninth inning. For me, the night was less successful. I never did get anything thrown my way; however, I did collect handouts given out as we left the ballpark, including a sample of Pert shampoo (the official brand of the Zephyrs) and a bag of Lay's new spicy ketchup potato chips.

Undoubtedly the big winner of the night was Maria. Not only did she go home with a ball, but also, in her mind it had been snared by Mom. No boy could top that.

CARNIVAL

Custer at Mardi Gras

Mardi Gras 1872, celebrities were coming to town. That was the year of the first Rex parade. The big name arrivals added to the luster. Lydia Thompson, the famous burlesque singer, would be making a return visit; so too would Lotta Crabtree, another of the generation of stage performers. Dan Rice, the most famous name in American circuses, was staging shows. Causing the most buzz, however, was the arrival of real royalty, the Russian Grand Duke Alexis Alexandrovich.

By then on the last leg of his United States tour, Alexis's presence at the first Rex parade, though coincidental, would add a touch of legitimate royalty to the day. Of all the people in town, however, the one whose name would become the best known over time was Alexis's military escort, General George Armstrong Custer.

Russians were of special interest in the United States of that era; not only because few people ever saw one, especially a Grand Duke, but because the United States had bought Alaska from that nation in 1867. The Russians were trade partners from a different world.

What interested Alexis most though were buffalo and Indians. The young Grand Duke (he was twenty-two) had read about the American West and wanted to experience it. At his request, President Grant had even ordered Custer to escort the Grand Duke on his American jaunt, the highlight of which was a government arranged buffalo hunt in Nebraska. Joining the two men at the camp that was set up for the duke were some of the top military brass as well as buffalo hunter and showman Buffalo Bill Cody, and an Indian chief named Spotted Tail.

New Orleans, though, was where the Grand Duke's visit would be best remembered. From Nebraska, the entourage took a steamboat down the Mississippi River, with a stop in St. Louis, and then on to New Orleans, arriving at a dock near what is now the intersection of South Carrollton Avenue and St. Charles Avenue.

For Custer, returning to New Orleans must have been a treat. He had visited the city before, most notably in May 1865, escorted by his wife Libbie. Here he was to meet with Army Commander Philip Sheridan.

Author Kevin Sullivan in his book *Custer's Road to Disaster: The Path to Little Bighorn* would write that New Orleans held "a great deal of fascination for the Custers." After dining in some of the city's restaurants, Libbie wrote that "we saw eating made a fine art." Custer, the union general, was enamored by the local coffee saying that even the best northern blend was "almost equal to the French Market."

By 1872 when Custer returned to New Orleans with Alexis, he did have some celebrity status as a hero of the Civil War Battle of Bull Run. (Though New Orleans had been a Confederate city, Union officers were part of the landscape in this town that was still under federal occupation.)

Mardi Gras that year was February 13, a historic day in the festival's history because of Rex's debut pa-rade. The Grand Duke and his entourage saw the parade from box seats at Gallier Hall. Earlier that week, the visitors were entertained with a dinner at the posh Jockey Club located near the site of the Fair Grounds Racetrack that would open that year. Horse racing was a topic that interested Custer. He owned several racehorses including one, Frogtown, which would race at the Fair Grounds later that season.

Since more information was written about the Grand Duke's schedule, we can assume that it also applied to Custer. They would have stayed at the St.

Charles Hotel, which was the city's most elegant place to stay. On Mardi Gras night, they would have moved to a series of parties and balls. Both were a witness to Rex's nativity.

From there, Alexis would return to Russia and obscurity; Custer would achieve immortality, ironically, because of his mortality.

America should have been a happier place in the summer of 1876. The nation, now united again from the Civil War, was only nine days away from celebrating the centennial of its Declaration of Independence, but on July 25, the country suffered a loss. Not only was General Custer's army entirely eliminated by a union of Indian tribes led by Chiefs Crazy Horse and Sitting Bull, but the bodies of the soldiers, sons of church-going American moms, were mutilated so as, the attackers believed, to deny them entry into Heaven.

News of the massacre, especially coming so close to the centennial celebration, created national outrage.

Also receiving the news, though from a distance, was the Grand Duke Alexis, now twenty-six. He too would have a military career, though his would befit someone whose dad was the czar. He would eventually be put in charge of the Russian Navy for which he was given credit for modernization. He was later blamed, however, for a key naval defeat. His last years were spent in Paris, away from the Russian Revolution. Curiously, though French in origin, Mardi Gras, was never an extravagant celebration in the French capitol. Most likely, it was New Orleans that provided him the best Carnival he had ever seen. Perhaps his friend General Custer also taught him to appreciate really good coffee.

When Rex Met Zulu: A Lundi Gras Evening

Lundi Gras 1999 had extra excitement to it, at least for those gathered at Riverwalk near the stage at Spanish Plaza where Rex, King of Carnival, and his entourage would soon be arriving.

What was different that year was the coming of special visitors, the Zulu King and his followers, who were on the way to greet Rex.

This moment oozed with significance, not just racially but symbolically. There was more news media than usual with cameras readied.

A reporter from a Los Angeles TV station even put a microphone in front of me to comment on the significance of the event. (Full disclosure, having been involved with the founding of the Lundi Gras ceremony I have served as emcee. My presence has been conspicuous by my purple, green, and gold *Cat in the Hat* type chapeau.)

Myron Moorehead, a physician, had been elected Zulu that year, and he played the role to the fullest, even creating events, including a party for other kings and staging a boat arrival that morning at Rivertown in Kenner. That would be his first of two water rides that day; the second would be downtown when he and his followers docked at Zulu's Lundi Gras party near the Aquarium. His biggest idea, however, would become one of Carnival's celebrated moments. It was he who suggested that on Lundi Gras Zulu should greet Rex.

Rex officials huddled. The idea was accepted. Rex, having stepped off a Coast Guard cutter, arrived at Riverwalk's stage at 6:00 p.m. First there were proclamations and gift exchanges, and then came the moment. The crowd was excited. Though everyone knew what was about to happen, we teased the crowd saying that a special visitor would be arriving soon. Moments later we provided more news: the mysterious guest was approaching. The crowd played along. There were chills down my spine when I finally announced: "Ladies and gentlemen, the visitor has arrived, please welcome King Zulu." The crowd, and it is relevant to the story to say that it was mostly white, went wild. Zulu added to the moment by being dressed in African motif. His followers wore the traditional gold blazers. The sight on stage was bejeweled with Rex (Louis Freeman) wearing the costume of a seafaring King and Zulu in feathery glory.

This is the type of moment that mayors crave. Carnival had delivered a love-in that City Hall never can. If it would have been proper, the two kings and mayor Marc Morial would have boogied on stage. Instead, they did a lot of handshaking and hugging.

From that moment, the tradition would evolve: the reigning Rex, Zulu, and mayor stood at the center of the stage and, after the crowd counted for from ten to one, pushed down a plunger which ignited a fireworks show over the river. (Incredibly, the only pyrotechnics display in Carnival.)

If Mardi Gras had a high, holy moment that was it. The *Louisiana Weekly,* a Black owned newspaper, would one day recall the evening in a feature on Zulu history:

> *Zulu helped create a significant milestone in New Orleans race relations in 1999, when the respective kings of the traditionally Black Zulu krewe and the traditionally White Rex krewe exchanged official greetings for the first time in history.*
>
> *This is history making," then-City Councilman and long-standing Zulu member Roy Glapion Jr. was quoted in reports as saying, "This has never taken place."*

History is made in many different ways. Sometimes it is even accompanied by fireworks over a river.

Momus and the Satirical Three

So many folks were mad at Momus that even the Governor had to get involved. He sent a telegram to Washington, DC hoping to sooth the frayed feelings.

In 1877 feelings were easily bruised. New Orleans, like the rest of the South, was suffering through the last days of Reconstruction. Carnival time generally provided an uneasy truce to the extent that the US Army band marched in parades, including Momus's of that year, and both the Army and the Navy greeted Rex when he arrived by river. But Momus, imp that he was, felt the need to level the barb at the federal occupiers and did so in a parade themed, "Hades–A Dream of Momus."

Not since Comus had raked the feds with an 1873 parade entitled "Missing Links of Darwin's Origins of the Species" had there been such satire. In that parade, President Grant had been depicted as an insect—a tobacco grub—and Union General Ben Butler was shown as a hyena.

Grant was spoofed in the Momus parade too—as the devil Beelzebub sitting on an imperial throne. The local agents of federal force were also teased, including General Butler who, along with Republican bosses, was displayed standing on a sinking ship in a sea of fire.

Momus marched. Tempers rose. On the next day there were demands for punishment. Perry Young, in his book, *The Mistick Krewe: Chronicles of Comus and Kin* reported that, the masker "who impersonated Beelzebub was told to his face that whoever travestied President Grant would be shot if identified."

Governor Francis T. Nicholls, no supporter of the occupiers but worried that their outrage would cause increased tension, fired off a telegram to the state's military representative in Washington: "The sentiment of the whole community is opposed to what happened at the celebration on Thursday."

Nicholls was diplomatic but wrong. Far from being opposed, much of the community was privately giggling. Even the Union General Uriah Pennypacker seemed less offended than others on his side and allowed the infantry to escort Rex on his arrival the following Monday.

Still, the seething continued. A Reconstruction publication called *The Official*

Journal of the State of Louisiana complained about the parade and added that it "is rumored that this is to be the last public display of Momus. We hope so out of respect for its dead fame."

There was a bit of truth to the statement. Momus survived but satire did not. "The Dream of Hades" turned out to be a nightmare. By informal understanding, krewes retreated to the other side of the controversy line. Satire–so naturally a part of a Carnival—was lost in New Orleans for one hundred years.

Then in 1977 the Knights of Momus surprised the city by bringing back the barb. There was a contemporary cast of characters to ridicule. In a new age of Carnival with super-krewes and towering floats, Momus was in danger of appearing to be a tired, old parade. The return to the barb recharged the group. Momus became a must-see for parade buffs as a rollicking gesture accompanying the king on his float and set the tone for what was to follow. Typical of the Knights' parade was the 1991 march that poked fun at a high-rolling Edwin Edwards and a befuddled Saddam Hussein. No one knew at the time that the laughing would soon stop.

Momus never paraded again after that year having retreated once more, this time in the face of a controversial city discrimination ordinance. The floats remained stored in the den with the images of Edwards and Saddam subject to cobwebs. But like the seeds from an aging tree that are carried by the wind and dropped on fertile soil, there were sprouts of the Momus spirit. First came an unlikely source in 1993, a short-lived Jefferson Parish transplant krewe known as Saturn that redefined itself after having secured a slot on St. Charles Avenue, Carnival's Broadway. Saturn developed a Momus look and a satirical wit sometimes as wicked as vintage Momus. Then in 1996, a new group formed, Le Krewe d'Etat—an organization so intent at satire that even its name is a devious pun. And making its debut in 2001, the Knights of Chaos, a group that has secured the use of the old Momus floats. So now, add in the Krewe of Tucks and the Vieux Carre based Krewe du Vieux and satirical parades have gone from none to one to at least five, the most ever. The ghost of the Momus parade survives.

Unfortunately, too many parade-goers may not see the ghost for the beads. In the old days, throws were occasional and sparse, the emphasis was on the design of the floats. Today the obsession is with catching as much as possible. In a true setback, krewes have even been rated not by the quality of their design but by the quantity of their throws.

Satirists will be challenged to deliver their punch lines through the seas of waving arms. But topical humor may be the way to make people pay more attention to floats as an art form.

Bringing wit back to Carnival: that would truly be a dream of Momus.

When Rex Met *Aida*

Cairo, Egypt, and New Orleans share the same latitude, thirty degrees, which makes both towns sort of steamy and subtropical—places where vegetation and the spirit sprout, even in the winter.

That was certainly the case in 1871 when an event in Egypt would forever become part of something that was germinating in New Orleans.

To celebrate the opening of the Suez Canal, the ruling khedive had commissioned an opera to be staged at the Cairo Opera House. Chosen as the composer was one of Europe's biggest names, the Italian, Giuseppe Verdi. After some delays, the premier performance was staged Christmas Eve of that year.

Appropriately Verdi's opera had an Egyptian theme set around the tragic story of a captured Ethiopian princess (Aida) who fell in love with an Egyptian military commander and the conflict that was caused with the pharaoh.

Verdi would compose a lavish opera filled with what would become some of the genre's most cherished music, none more so than the stunning piece that was performed in act II, scene two. Beginning with the blare of trumpets, a cast of seemingly hundreds, many dressed as soldiers, royalty, and plain Egyptian folks moved in procession across the stage to the stirring sounds of what was to be known as the "Triumphal March" or more commonly the "Grand March" from *Aida.* Never had music captured the spirit of triumph more than Verdi's masterpiece march. If opera was war, Egypt could have ruled the world.

That same month in New Orleans, a group of young men was having meetings at the St. Charles Hotel. Like Verdi, they too were on a mission to create something new, in this case it was a parade that would debut only a few weeks later on February 13, Mardi Gras, 1872. There already were two Carnival parades, the Mistick Krewe of Comus and Twelfth Night Revelers, but they marched at night, bookends to the season, one on its first day, the other on its last. The new parade would be different. It would be held during the day and part of its mission would be to unite the various miscellaneous maskers that strolled the streets on Mardi Gras into one organized parade. The ruler would be the people's monarch to be referred to as "The King of Carnival," or more simply, borrowing from the Latin word for king, "Rex."

His Majesty's first parade was in itself a triumphal march. So much so that the procession became an annual event, eventually to include its own ball on the evening of Mardi Gras where a debutante, to be known as the "Queen of Carnival," would promenade with Rex around the floor.

Back in Europe, *Aida* was a major hit performed in the continent's grandest theaters. The opera reached the United States in November, 1872 when it was performed at the Academy of Music in Manhattan. Though New Orleans was a major opera center, the Verdi composition, according to local opera historian Jack Belsom, was not performed here until December 6, 1879 at the French Opera House by the touring Strakosch Italian Opera Company. "Thus it was sung in the original Italian rather than in French." Belsom says. "It was sung a total of three times that season but was not enthusiastically received because of less than adequate singers and décor.

"Things changed drastically the following season (1880-81) when the excellent de Beauplan French troupe was in residence," Belsom added. "They gave *Aida* a spectacular production, the sets based on designs from the original premiere, and with a strong cast. The first staging was on December 16, 1880, and it was done often that season, to acclaim."

That season created the setting for a most unusual opera incident: Mardi Gras, 1881 was on March 1. According to Belsom's research, Rex had special plans for the night before: "The papers reported that on the previous evening (February 28) during a performance of *Aida*, Rex made an appearance at the French Opera House in mid-performance. Before the third act was over, being escorted to the royal box by de Beauplan, a guard of honor, and lackeys with torches, to rounds of applause, and the royal anthem 'If Ever I Cease to Love' which the orchestra struck up." Thus when Rex and *Aida* first met, Rex's anthem, for the first and only time, was injected into Verdi's Nile scene.

(Perhaps inspired by the opera the next year, in 1882, when the Krewe of Proteus made its debut, the ball theme was "Egyptian Mythology.")

There is one more date to this saga and that is Mardi Gras evening, 1882. That's when the Rex Organization and the Mistick Krewe of Comus first staged what would become familiarly known as "the Meeting of the Courts." We do not know for sure what music was played but we do know that by that year, the "Triumphal March" was a hot number perfect for such occasions.

We do know that in modern times Rex responds to two marches, his own, "If Ever I Cease to Love" and the march from *Aida*, as he and Comus and their queens circle the floor in what is Carnival society's high holy moment.

By circumstance, Rex and *Aida* are contemporaries, having made their debuts only fifty-one days apart in different parts of the world but along the same latitude, and each in recognition of ceremony and royalty. And their triumphs continue.

When Rex Met *Aida:* More to the Story

Editor's note: The previous article waxed on about the parallels between the debut of the Rex organization in Feb. 13,1872 and the first performance, in Cairo, on Christmas Eve, 1871 of the opera Aida *whose moving grand march would traditionally be performed during the Rex/Comus balls. Now, there's more to the story:*

Over one hundred and thirty years ago, one of the most bizarre events in the history of opera took place in New Orleans—the reign of a fictitious Pharaoh was temporally interrupted by a then contemporary ceremonial king, and the music of each blended.

Mardi Gras, 1881 was on March 1. According to Belsom's research, Rex had special plans for the night before: "The papers reported that on the previous evening (February 28) during a performance of *Aida,* Rex made an appearance at the French Opera House in mid-performance. Before the third act was over, being escorted to the royal box by de Beauplan, a guard of honor, and lackeys with torches, to rounds of applause, and the royal anthem 'If Ever I Cease to Love' which the orchestra struck up." Thus when Rex and *Aida* first met, Rex's anthem, for the first and only time, was injected into Verdi's Nile scene.

In the world of Carnival, Rex is a powerful monarch—that incident showed just how powerful. He was able to interrupt an opera with the obvious support of the event's organizers. One might suspect, as is true today, that the men of Rex were on many important boards, including in this case, having some stroke in the theater.

For whatever the connections might have been, *Aida's* presence seemed to have touched off a bout of Egyptian Mania around town.

A year later, in 1882, when the Krewe of Proteus made its debut, the ball's theme was "Egyptian Mythology."

One more curiosity: Depending on who is doing the counting, the debuts of *Aida* and Rex are even closer than originally believed. Giuseppe Verdi did not consider the Cairo performance to be the official premiere. He protested that the event was a closed affair and not open to the public. To Verdi, the real premiere was when his opera opened at the glistening La Scala opera house in Milan. Not only were there general tickets sales but, unlike in the Cairo presentation, superstar Teresa Stolz, an operatic hot number who Verdi had in mind when he wrote the lead role, performed. The date of that event was February 8, 1872, five days before the Rex debut.

Historic parallels are little more than a collection of trivia without learning from them. The sagas of *Aida* and Rex give a glimpse of sense of style among the better-educated men of the Victorian age. Schooled in the classics and raised with a sense of mission, their life was also filled with battles. *Aida,* the character, suffered from slavery, lost love, discrimination, and war. The men of Rex, living in a period still referred to as "Reconstruction" had in the previous decade experienced the hardships of a great civil war. Now was the time for peace and civility. For the moment two rivers, the Nile and the Mississippi, flowed as one.

Parades in Quarter Time

A winter night, now long ago, in the Vieux Carré, there was that Carnival-like edge in the streets. The plea of the vendors echoed off the old buildings through the narrow streets. Parallel lines of people stood alongside the curbs as though to form a path for the awaited procession. Occasionally, a head from the crowd would bob over the street, the eyes turned to the left to determine if the parade was coming.

Fate this night, and I don't remember why, brought me to the spot on Orleans Street where the parades made the last leg of their journey through the Quarter before crossing North Rampart and heading for adjournment at the Municipal Auditorium. It would be my first view of a parade from that vantage point. I didn't know at the time that it would also be my last.

In the year to follow, some folks in City Hall would issue a decree forever banning most Carnival parades from the streets of the Quarter. Some of the newer parades had become too big for the neighborhood to handle, so all must suffer. At that moment, as I was among those waiting in anticipation of the blinking lights that precede each march, I was experiencing a transitional moment, the dawn of the passage from what Carnival was.

Parades turned from Royal Street toward the auditorium at the back of St. Anthony's Garden, the small park behind St. Louis Cathedral. At the 500 block of Royal, television station WDSU would place a camera on its balcony, recording the parades for showing after the news. Mel Leavitt, local TV's first star, did the narration. That view of Carnival, in black and white through a camera's lens, was the angle that most people saw of parades in the Quarter. Being there live in the streets added not only color but the awesome framework of the Vieux Carré. The parades of that day were built as though to be in scale with the neighborhood. As seen from the streets, the parade and the surroundings meshed, a blast of color and antiquity.

Suddenly those in the crowd received their cue. The blinking lights were turning from Royal onto Orleans. It wasn't long before the full parade was approaching. The scene was of old floats waddling along, their shimmering papier-mâché flowers being illuminated by the gold haze from the flambeaux. The beat of the bands and the cries from the crowd ricocheting along the street added to the sensory overflow. But then I noticed something else: In the background, a floodlight placed in front of the Christ statue in St. Anthony's Garden cast the shadow of the figure, in towering proportions, on the back of the cathedral. The figure's hands were outstretched as though it, too, wanted to catch beads.

An official from the fire department said at a meeting that the parades should forever be banned from the Quarter because of the hazard they create. To make sure, a prohibition had even been encoded in a city ordinance. "Besides," the official asked, "what was the big deal about parades in the Quarter anyway?" Years later in the memories of Leavitt's life, there were clips of the vintage broadcasts from the days when television was young, and Carnival paraded where it should be. Today, there are still folks in the crowds looking for the parades to come. But there are other heads turned in the opposite direction, yearning for the Carnivals that have passed.

Bacchus Stories

What do you do when your star says he is freezing? The answer: whatever he wants.

That was the situation on the night of the first Bacchus parade, February 16, 1969. With great fanfare, this new parading organization, to which the title of "Super Krewe" would later be given by the original Rex Duke parade critic, was set to role with its thrilling innovations: huge floats and a bona fide celebrity as king. That celebrity was movie star Danny Kaye, who through the magic of someone connected with Bacchus knowing someone, who knew someone, who knew Kaye, agreed to the gig.

Kaye, dressed in fine Bacchanal regalia, was escorted on to the float and to his throne. It was a fine moment as adoring crowd members looked on. There was only one problem. Though the evening was warm with enthusiasm, the night was frigid. The king complained. He needed to be warmed. The officers of the new krewe, skilled with the machinations of putting a parade together, faced a new issue—how to heat a throne, and to do it quickly?

Would Bacchus be toasty, or would he be iced? More later.

Heating his highness would be the first of many issues the krewe members would face through the decades. One year the reigning Bacchus, despite his mighty powers, could not delay nature. He had to make a run. At Gallier Hall he was escorted off the float long enough to stop at the nearest restroom. Flushed with relief, he soon returned to the throne for a worry-free ride.

One year, the reigning Bacchus was toasted by another krewe as his float sided up to a Canal Street hotel. Only, the toasting Krewe was a bit too generous with its pouring of champagne so that Bacchus's royal knees were wobbly by the time he addressed his subjects at the convention center.

Another Bacchus, facing domestic discord, carried his misery with him. He was grumpy throughout his ride and showed it.

Most Bacchuses have reigned problem-free and joyfully, though they are not the only source of sparkle. The oversized floats have increasingly competed for star power with the man of the throne. The tandem float, the one with several units connected, increased the size of the pageantry. Their passing is big and boisterous though their creation goes back to a quiet moment.

August Perez, one of the Bacchus founders and a former krewe captain, was flying out of New Orleans. As the plane waited on the tarmac, he noticed the wagons pulling luggage carts and how each cart turned at the same spot where the previous one had. Ideas began to click and the idea of a float, designed with a similar turning mechanism evolved. Such floats are now in all the Super Krewes but their roots trace back to suitcases being delivered.

There was a delivery heading to Kaye that first Bacchus night. Owen "Pip" Brennan Jr., the krewe's founding captain, would recall that someone found a heater and was able to rig it up near the throne. Kaye was satisfied. Then the parade started. As the float turned onto the street, the king was thrilled with the thousands of people waiting to see him. He stood up and gracefully waved his scepter. After that, Kaye hardly sat down, Brennan recalled. He forgot all about the cold as the little heater aimed its air at an empty throne.

Lesson learned that night: there is nothing as warm as the cheer of a crowd.

Year of the Strike

In 1979, New Orleans and its Carnival faced a crisis together. Both would be enriched by the experience though there would be plenty of pain and stress along the way.

At issue were the New Orleans Police who had threatened to go on strike just in time for that season's parades. Without the police there could be no security; without the security there could be no parades. To say that "Mardi Gras would be cancelled" was inaccurate because the day on the calendar would still exist, but without its most visible manifestation: the parades; the season, some feared, would be wrecked.

Dutch Morial was the mayor at the time, having been sworn in the previous May. It is relevant to the story that Morial was the city's first Black mayor. Though there had been some concessions made to the police on a pay increase, they wanted more, particularly bargaining rights. Morial was adamant in opposing that, arguing that the city would lose control of the department and its finances. At first there was concern if the White population of New Orleans would support a Black mayor against the police department, but as the parade season drew closer the police side made blunders. One was the arrival of a Teamster Union official from Detroit to be a speaker for the police. With his open collar and gold chain the official conjured no esteem. Then there were local strike leaders who talked about wrecking the city. At a rally a toy stuffed rabbit was shown lynched, suggesting that after killing Mardi Gras the strikers would do the same for Easter.

Then came the cavalry. In one of the great moments in the city's civic history, the krewe leaders stood together before a TV camera announcing that they were not going to parade. The Rex captain spoke for most krewes, saying they "would not be held hostage by the Teamsters Union."

A few krewes, mostly newer ones, did parade in Jefferson Parish that year, but other krewes, especially the older ones, the groups guided by tradition, stayed off the street. To them they could not parade anywhere else but in New Orleans.

Mardi Gras was February 9 that year, and with the tension of the parades removed there was still celebrating. The French Quarter was a happy place resembling an urban street festival. The mood was peaceful but, just in case, National Guard soldiers stood ready at various intersections. These young men protected the city while girls danced in front of them, some placing flowers in their helmets. From the balconies, they saw sights that basic training had just not prepared them for.

By the next day, the police strike was in the ashes. With Carnival over, the police had lost their leverage and the strike fell apart. The Teamsters went home. It was a victory for Morial and the city which still controlled its own police department.

Years later, a Black history professor, who was also a friend of Moral's, told me how hard the situation had been with the mayor. As a lawyer he had been sympathetic to unions and represented their causes, but at this time he had to stand against them for the civic good.

Because he was Black, there was speculation that as mayor, Morial would not look kindly on Carnival and its mostly White krewes. But the strike solidified the relationships. As though in gratitude for the backing, he was a very supportive mayor.

Contrary to rumors about continuing the ill will, by the next year, 1980, the parades were back in full groove. On the last night of the season, there was a ceremony that was touching, though few people saw. The Comus parade still rolled and closed out the season. Traditionally, mayors toast the parades at Gallier Hall. That night, the Comus parade included a battery of New Orleans motorcycle police. At Gallier Hall they got off their cycles to receive glasses of champagne. And then the police and the mayor, enemies a year earlier, toasted each other.

All was good and the spirit of Carnival had prevailed.

Herbert Jahncke: A Royal Artist

Float Number Two in the 2006 parade of Mobile's Mystics of Time depicted a serpent winding down the street. The float was gorgeous with radiant colors spotting the monster's trunk and blasts of fiery yellow radiating from its mouth.

Carnivals in Mobile and in New Orleans have historic links; one of the last of those links was float builder Herbert Jahncke who, in 2007, also built the parades of Proteus, Le Krewe d'Etat, Hermes, and Chaos in New Orleans. To most of the spectators in Mobile that night, their thoughts were probably lost to the sight of the flashy snake and to their passion for beads. It would take a person of rare artistic grasp to think like the creators of the very first Comus parade in New Orleans whose theme "The Demon Actors in Milton's Paradise Lost" also explored the unexplained.

Such a person would have been Jahncke, who appreciated the history and style of the early Carnival and who knew that demons and serpents make compelling street art.

Herbert Jahncke was the son of a prominent Northshore family whose business was best known for workboat services and dredging. His passion, though, was floats more than boats. He was enamored by the New Orleans Mardi Gras and at that, he achieved nobility since his father reigned as Rex in 1966.

Jahncke could have been a high-powered business executive but instead he wanted to build Carnival floats for a living. His company, Royal Artists, specialized in designs more in keeping with the early Carnival. In an age of super-sized floats, Jahncke appreciated the scale of the early parades.

Proteus was one of Jahncke's masterpieces, with his crowning achievement perhaps being the 2006 parade that celebrated the old-line krewe's 125th anniversary. Each float represented a theme from Proteus's past, thus unleashing a menagerie of radiant fish and fanciful creatures moving in succession, like a stream of salmon, up the parade route.

That same year, Hermes's rendition of the "Voyages of Ulysses" included a scene in which the explorer wrestled a float–long green serpent whose head lurched across his shoulder.

Newest to Jahncke's stable was Le Krewe d'Etat. Because the parade was satirical it presented unique challenges, particularly depicting contemporary topical figures for which, unlike Ulysses, there is certainty about what they look like. Jahncke's sculpture work was dead-on, including a likeness of then Ray Nagin that could be no more exact had the mayor looked in a mirror.

Chaos presented another challenge. Using the floats and style of the former Momus parade, the Knights also specialize in topical humor through more in the traditional cartoonish style. In the first Mardi Gras after Katrina, one float teased Jefferson Parish and the pumping stations that were ordered abandoned even as the streets flooded. Parish President Aaron Broussard was depicted as a Humpty Dumpty character teetering atop a wall.

Herbert Jahncke was a nice man with a graying beard and lots of stories to tell. His promise to one day take me on a boat trip down the Tchefunctre River will unfortunately go unfulfilled. He died December 4, 2007. (In the context of his passions, that day was significant because it was exactly two months before the next Proteus parade.) His loss to the New Orleans Carnival and to the preservation of its art is enormous. In life as in Mardi Gras we are presented with occasional demons. Blessed are those who bring joy along the route.

When Zulu Saved Mardi Gras

During the bad days of 2006 shortly after Katrina, Mayor Ray Nagin went to Atlanta where he met with a group of Black displaced New Orleanians. The crowd had the concerns that might be expected with their lives uprooted and the city's future uncertain. Nagin tried to answer as best as he could. But what the night would be best remembered for was that toward the end of the questioning one woman raised her hand and scolded that with so many people displaced nobody should be thinking about having Mardi Gras parades. Nagin, perhaps caught off guard, agreed.

His Honor might not have been thinking about the television cameras in the back of the room or the immediacy of modern communication or of the significance of his nod to the affirmative, but by the ten o'clock news that Sunday night the lead story in New Orleans was that the mayor was saying that there should be no Carnival celebration.

Coming at a time when the world's media were still camped in the city, the statement was flashed internationally and presented as another example of a city so down on its knees that it could not stage a parade. New Orleans without Mardi Gras—perhaps the city was really dead.

After returning to New Orleans, it did not take long for the mayor to change his position. Saying he was "outvoted" by the tourist commission, Nagin said he favored a modified parade schedule. (My research of the city charter has failed to discover any clause under which the tourist commission can outvote the mayor, but I think I understood his point.)

Now the trick was in how to modify the schedule. Most parades would have fewer floats and their routes would be shortened. For many krewes, smaller was good because they barely had the strength to put together anything. One group that was quite vocal, however, especially about the route shortening was Zulu. Its officers spoke passionately about being allowed to parade in those neighborhoods with cultural links to the group. Zulu roared. It wanted to be on the streets with its full integrity.

There was dissension within the Zulu organization. One past king threatened to sue, saying it was inappropriate for the group to march. But the Zulu bosses were undeterred.

In the end Zulu got its way.

In 2009, Zulu celebrated its centennial. Within that century, Zulu has had few grander, or more important, moments than in that first Carnival after Katrina. Imagine had Zulu not paraded: With so much media attention and with the very faint heartbeat of the city being overly analyzed the word would have spread around the globe: White people parading while Black people suffer.

Truth is there were lots of White folks suffering too, including many that feebly climbed on floats, some that were decorated with blue tarpaulins to spoof the recovery.

By taking a stand, Zulu saved Carnival in 2006 and perhaps forevermore. Once the parades started, the message was spread that there was still life and joy in this battered city that had risen from its knees if only to yell, "Throw me something!" Anyone who paid attention might have learned that Carnival is not about racial divides but multiple cultures celebrating in their own way. With Zulu on the march the Mardi Gras Indians could prowl their neighborhoods with a little more spirit, the bars in Treme could put beer on ice.

And those people in Atlanta, I suspect they celebrated too. Mardi Gras provides a good excuse to come home, if only for a day. When water rises, coconuts still float.

The Greatest Mardi Gras Ever

Mardi Gras was on February 28 in 2006. The late date was fortunate because the Katrina-battered city needed every extra day it could get to prop itself up for the celebration it needed to have. Since March 3, 1699, the amazingly coincidental date when Frenchmen first camped out in what would be Louisiana territory on a date that happened to be Mardi Gras; there had been 306 celebrations of some sort each year in the city. Mardi Gras 2006 was going to be the most important of all. It wasn't about partying, economic development, or tradition; it was about a city believing in itself again.

Naysayers said their nays about cancelling Carnival activities, nevertheless, Throughout the city the chant was heard—folks wanted Mardi Gras. There was concern that if we celebrated too hard the rest of the world would think we did not need help; others argued that if we did not celebrate the world would see the city as being lifeless. Most of all, folks said they just needed Carnival, including the Krewe of Zulu, whose voice resonated in the Black community by assuring that it would be strutting on Mardi Gras.

For most krewes, the task was not easy. Some did not parade; some combined with others to create hybrid parades in which many floats had blue tarps—the roof material seen around town and a symbol of the rebuilding.

On the Saturday before Mardi Gras, weather played havoc, so much so that the krewe of Endymion had to postpone, deciding instead to make the logistically challenging move of parading behind Bacchus the next night.

Lundi Gras went smoothly with Rex, Tabasco magnate Paul McIlhenny, arriving by river to take reign over his wrecked but regal empire.

With fireworks splashing overhead, Rex looked out from Riverwalk toward the towers of downtown. Only six months earlier, there had been the frightening howl of winds whipping through the canyons of buildings. On this night there was the echo of drumbeats.

Zulu led the activity on Mardi Gras morning being true to its commitment to parade. The real test though, would be Rex who took seriously his title as the "King of Carnival." If any parade had to be at full stride, it needed to be this one. The challenge was formidable. The Rex den had been battered by the storm and its high waters. Some of its old floats are built on wagon beds that still have wooden-spoked wheels. If there is a profession that is in short supply, it is wheelwrights capable of fixing such damages. Rex organizers searched the nation to find who they needed.

Celebrating a theme of "Beaux Arts and Letters" Rex turned onto the street and presented a beautiful, full capacity parade. There would be no water stains or mold marks in the kingdom of Rex.

Like a herd of peacocks, the Society of St. Anne added more color to the French Quarter as its hundreds of maskers sauntered their way from Bywater toward Canal Street. Within its ranks, lies the true spirit of Carnival, which cannot be detained and is easily unleashed. Just as in 1979 when a very tense strike by police caused all parades to be cancelled, Mardi Gras, the day itself, could not be denied. Celebrating hard was more than an escape—it was a mission.

Overall, the crowd was a little smaller than usual, partially because some hotels had not reopened and partially because many people still thought New Orleans was underwater. Instead, the city played in the sun. Adding to the splendor was the weather that peaked at seventy-six degrees and a cloudless sky.

That night, Rex and Comus continued their Meeting of the Courts ritual before their invited guests and a TV audience. Carnival reached its final moment as the monarchs left the Court.

I wondered if there had ever been a Carnival day when the weather was better. Maybe I could check old records I thought, having conceded that this search was beyond Google capacity. But then I realized that the weather had been perfect, and perfection could not be improved upon. Add to it the emotional lift given to a city that so recently had been flattened and this was, no doubt, the greatest Mardi Gras ever.

Ash Wednesday and its somber message could wait. The spirit of rebirth had captured the day.

The Throw

At 7:14 p.m. Marty's arm acted as a pivot sending a stash of throws from his spot on the float toward the crowd standing along the St. Charles Avenue sidewalk. An instantaneous jerk of the float caused the throw to be erratic. From his bag Marty had pulled five pairs of beads and two doubloons. By 7:14:01 the stash was ascending toward the apex of its arch before beginning its descent. The jerking motion had caused the different items to take varying directions so that one doubloon's course was toward a storm drain at the curb. The other doubloon gained a bit more trajectory and was heading toward a crash landing on the sidewalk.

For the beads, the aerodynamics was different so that by 7:14:02 three pairs seemed to briefly hover over the crowds as hands reached mercilessly to snatch them.

By 7:14:03 the throws had experienced their first fatality. An errant pair of beads had been grabbed, at each end, simultaneously by a hand from two different people. Each person, unwilling to concede their catch to the other, yanked at the plastic necklace hoping to capture it but instead causing the string to break and for its individual beads, having made the long trip from China, to end their journey by bouncing unnoticed on the sidewalk only to be mindlessly stomped on by those in pursuit of other rewards.

Fate was no better for one of the doubloons, which, by 7:14:05 had ricocheted into the drain, never to be seen again. The other doubloon twirled on its edge momentarily once it hit the sidewalk until it was stomped on by a parade-goer who kept it imprisoned under his boot.

Of all the missiles launched by Marty on this winter night, the greatest journey was that of one big-beaded necklace that the float's sudden jerk had propelled toward the sky. It might have reached the stars had it not been abruptly snagged by a branch from an overhanging oak tree. The throw's impact, however, was forceful enough, that, by 7:14:09, it caused another pair of beads, which had been captured by the tree a year earlier to be dislodged and to fall around the neck of Hector, a resident at the nearby Salvation Army facility, who was witnessing his first Carnival parade. Hector was both stunned and delighted at his sudden fortune.

By 7:15 the float that carried Marty was two blocks down the street and the booty from his toss was largely forgotten as barrages from other floats reached the crowd. Of Marty's throws, three captured pairs of beads were put in a bag with the catcher's intent to toss them again in the St. Patrick's Day parade. The surviving doubloon was eventually lifted from beneath the boot and later that evening placed in a shoebox filled with a decade's worth of other doubloons.

Hector's pair of beads was faded, and its string frayed but it was prized jewelry to him. He draped it on a lamp near his bunk that night and it would forever travel with him wherever he went.

By most measures, the journey of Marty's bounty had taken about two seconds except for the pair of beads now dangling from a tree. Its fate was now up to the wind, or to the oncoming throws from the next parade.

Year Of the Non-Pirate

If you see a pirate this Mardi Gras, don't call my name because it won't be me. Most often in recent years I have dressed like a rogue from the seas for several reasons:

I have by now collected a bag full of pirate-like costume parts.

Pirate costumes are not too cumbersome, possibly because the pirates often had to make quick getaways.

When you meet another pirate coming down the street on Mardi Gras, they often go, "Arrrggghhh!" I reply with a similar response, which is about as deep in conversation as I want to get with a passing pirate.

Though no one confuses me for Johnny Depp, I do get to wear a Jack Sparrow, *Pirates of the Caribbean,* wig.

I also get to wear one of those cool tri-cornered hats.

Nevertheless, my act has gotten stale. "Not a pirate again?" an acquaintance would say. I could have countered by saying, "No, I am a privateer," but that is so UNO no one would believe it.

One year, with the help of a friend who is a great costume maker, a new costume was made. Thinking ahead to the city's Tricentennial in 2018, I intended to be Bienville. The costume was great, complete with a vest and breeches made with gold-colored fabric, but the tri-corner hat did me in. I could have been George Washington, but people still saw me as a pirate, albeit a well-dressed one.

Bienville will make an appearance again on another Mardi Gras, but this is the year I have to break the pirate image totally.

For a Twelfth Night party I searched through a costume shop not wanting to get one of those velveteen pre-made costumes of Dracula or a medieval executioner, but hoping I could find parts from which a new costume would be fashioned. I was about to give up when I spotted a pilot's helmet like the type that the early aces such as the Red Baron wore. I bought that and a pair of optional flight goggles. There was no pilot jacket per se, but there were camouflage shirts that had nothing to do with flying but that when combined with the helmet and goggles looked like something that might have been worn during a dogfight over Prussia. All aces wore a long scarf. I grabbed one from a selection near the helmets. So there I had it. No one could confuse this costume for a pirate. Then I noticed that the scarf I had picked was green. Once I wrapped it around my neck I pronounced myself to be the Green Baron.

At that Twelfth Night party most all of the other costumes were far better than mine, but the getup did earn a certain amount of positive reaction if for no other reason than it was not a pirate. One woman, who actually is a pilot, was especially impressed with it.

So, this Mardi Gras the Green Baron will be patrolling the streets of the French Quarter. And should he meet another flying ace the response will be obvious, "Arrrggghhh!"

Harold Myers: The Passion of a Fan

Harold Myers loved Carnival in New Orleans and he celebrated it in a way unlike anyone else. He did not ride in a krewe and never reigned as a king, but he did capture the spirit and integrity of the season better than anyone else.

Myers's moment was on the evening of Twelfth Night. He and his accomplices would gather their trench coats, float riders' masks, a cowbell or two plus their hand-printed signs, and head out to the Willow Street streetcar barn. Once disguised they would congregate near the spot where the Phunny Phorty Phellows were preparing for their annual January 6 Streetcar ride to announce the Carnival season's arrival. One member of Myers' group would start ringing the bell, others held the signs, soon members of the Phellows would be drawn to the maskers whose identity they did not know.

Over the years, an informal routine evolved. "I didn't catch your names," some Phellow would say, to which the maskers would introduce themselves with names such as "Mokana," "Okeanos," and "Proteus." The signs they carried were satirical, some with a biting wit, some with an eerie inside knowledge of some of the Phellows.

Once the Phellows' streetcar ride began, the "Mystery Maskers," as the Phellows referred to them, would disappear showing up again generally at other spots along the route, each time with different signs. Then one year, a masker straddled the streetcar tracks as the trolley approached Gallier Hall. His sign boldly commanded the streetcar to stop. It did and thus began an annual ritual of Phellows officialdom and the Maskers toasting each other in front of Carnival's capitol.

One year the Maskers gave the Phellows a proclamation commanding that a plaque should be placed on the corner of Julia and Magazine Street stating that that was the spot where, in 1857, the first Comus parade began, and thus the beginning of the Carnival parading tradition.

Another year Zulu and his queen were among the Phellows' guests. Extending his arm through the window, the lead masker handed the Zulu royals cups of champagne for a trackside toast. The ritual was always brief. Within moments, the Phellows were climbing back into the streetcar, but not before one Phellow, always moved by the occasion, would tell the maskers, "Y'all are the real thing, you represent the true spirit of Carnival."

That ritual, which just evolved over years, was genuine, lasting nearly fifteen years, and amazingly, no one in the Phellows ever knew who the maskers were.

I was sitting in the waiting area at JFK Airport checking my messages. A saddened voice asked me to call saying that he had disturbing news about someone I had never met but that I was familiar with. That's when I found out about Harold Myers. On the evening before, Myers had been returning home from a Zephyrs' baseball game. His automobile was near Bonnabel Boulevard and the I-10 Service Road when a truck that had been stolen and was being pursued by the police crashed into him. The spirit was gone. His family's tragedy was one of Carnival's great losses.

"Harold loved virtually everything about New Orleans, the people, the food, the culture, the history, and often remarked that this city was unlike any other city in the world. He was emblematic of everything that was right about the city of New Orleans and unfortunately died being a tragic symbol of everything that was wrong with the city of New Orleans," one of his cousins wrote me.

I would learn that he worked for the Louisiana Department of Labor's Jobs Service where he was known for showing a real passion for outcasts and creating opportunities for them. A friend lamented that he would have wanted to find a job for the person who was driving the stolen truck.

When he last toasted the Phellows on Twelfth Night '09, Myers was told that the plaque he had proclaimed years earlier now existed. Though it speaks of Comus, the plaque, on the side of a building at Magazine and Julia Streets is a tribute to someone who appreciated Carnival not as a profiteer or even a celebrity, but as someone who was truly moved by the spirit in a way that few people understood.

Harold Myers lived in Metairie, but his funeral mass was at St. John the Baptist Catholic Church in Central City which, a cousin of his said, was his favorite church. "Why a church so far away from home?" I asked. "Because," the cousin answered, "it was close to the parade route."

Ash Wednesday

I once worked in an office where on the day after Mardi Gras, I noticed the two girls at the front desk each had ashen crosses on their forehead. At first, I thought it was touching that they had gone to church where, by tradition, the priest would make the appropriate smudge to remind followers of the somber message that to dust we shall return.

By their giggles, I sensed that the girls were not affected by the piety of the day, especially when I realized that both smoked and each has blessed the other with the char from their ashtray.

To me, Ash Wednesday's message is not as much about returning to dust but reclaiming reality, and there is a certain spirituality in that too. We in New Orleans are a blessed people to live in a place with European and Caribbean charm but with United States strength and amenities. Add to that a season when masking in the streets is encouraged; where we beg for baubles just for the sheer numbers; where the litter piles sparkle with beads, and where the rhythm is often that of our native music. It must be that too much of this experienced all the time certainly should be sinful. But there is Ash Wednesday to remind us that a life of feasting needs moments of fasting.

There was a time when, according to tradition, the ashes smudged on by the priests on Good Friday came from burning the leftover palms from Palm Sunday. Now slivers have replaced the full palms and the ash stash, I suspect, is down. Life changes: Many of the old churches are closed; there are fewer priests. Yet we celebrate with more persistence and fervor than ever, all the more to remember the counter-balancing message. We are denied little in our lives.

A smudge on Ash Wednesday could be a spiritual message or perhaps a splash of makeup that survived removal. Either way, we need to find peace with our body and our soul. Jazz Fest, after all, is never too far away.

FOOD

Banana Troubles

Here's a tip: If ever you are conducting a business deal with a man who is on a bike, and who is carrying a machete, and who speaks a different language than you do, be sure to get his cell phone number.

There will be no banana harvest at my home this season. For years, despite my doomed efforts to grow citrus and vegetables in the backyard, all that did grow was the bounty from the three banana trees that were planted long before I moved into the house. One year, my yard was a banana factory turning out bunches seemingly faster that I could whack them off the tree (note: for that, I carry a machete too) and in far greater numbers than for which there was demand.

There were still bunches bursting out as late as December, when the weather turned cold, really cold. The citrus bushes survived the several below-freezing nights, but not the banana trees, which turned into an ugly, jagged, brown curtain that was spread across the back fences.

Getting rid of them would be a mighty task for which I was thinking about having to hire a professional tree removal company with big trucks and hungry buzz saws, but then came Samuel, on his bike.

He approached me one morning as I was getting the newspaper. Samuel is Hispanic, and I am a fan of Hispanic laborers because without them I would still be living in my Katrina exile. I had no doubt about his work ethic or his skill with a machete, but I was concerned about how he would get rid of the debris. Our different accents did not always connect, but I understood enough to know that I should go to Home Depot to buy some industrial sized trash bags. As long as the debris was bagged, he explained, the garbage collectors would willingly take them.

Never one to argue with a man carrying a machete, Samuel and I had a deal. He pedaled away and came back shortly with a helper, a lean fellow wearing a straw Stetson hat who immediately began swinging Samuel's machete at the trees.

When I got home that evening, I noticed two things; one was how bare that backyard looked without the tropical backdrop, and the other was how full the front curb looked with two dozen or so forty-five-gallon industrial strength bags of banana tree pieces.

That's when I called Samuel on his cell phone. I wanted his assurance that the garbage collectors would take the bags. Our languages collided again, but he sounded like a man with inside knowledge. I should believe in the garbage truck.

As I went to get the newspaper the next morning, I heard a grinding noise outside accompanied by the yells of men. I sheepishly looked out the window, from which I could see the garbage truck stopped in front of the house, blocking traffic, while three men laboriously pulled the bags to the back of the truck. The bags were heavy, and the men were struggling. I did not know what the protocol was, but I hurried outside to give each worker a tip just as they were tossing the last loose stalk into the truck. The man who seemed to be in charge explained the rule that they should only take bagged items up to sixty pounds. My collection, according to the truck's scales, totaled about four hundred pounds. Oops. "The next time you do this . . ." the man started to explain. "There won't be a next time," I interrupted assuredly.

Without the banana trees, I have noticed, there is more sunlight in the backyard, and that might work to the benefit of the citrus plants. If there is one thing certain about banana trees, it is that they will grow back, though I am not sure if I want three. One will be enough to satisfy the primal feeling that comes with swinging a machete through a stem to liberate a ripened banana bunch.

There was one brief benefit to the neighborhood from the experience. Just as fragrant scents are sprayed to fumigate French Quarter streets, gushes of tree water splashed on our street as the truck's jaws crushed each bag. For the moment, the block was banana flavored. Winter had not been all-cruel.

~~~~~~

A Different Fig

~~~~~~

To me, the measure of any self-respecting New Orleans-based fig tree is if it can produce fruit by July Fourth. That was always the case with the most common local variety, the Celeste, whose produce seemed programmed to turn purple by Independence Day.

Katrina created new gardening opportunities. There is a space behind my house that I never knew what to do with until the storm knocked over the neighbor's cypress tree, whose shady expanse had prohibited anything from growing there. With the sun now free to zoom in, and in the spirit of the recovery, I wanted to plant trees that would provide food, not so much for the bounty but as a sign of revival—a once empty spot creating nourishment.

My first planting was going to be a Celeste fig tree, which would be the centerpiece of what I now call "the grove." But in those days after Katrina, the plant nurseries were not well supplied. Among the fig trees there were no Celestes, but something called a Kadota, at the time an ungainly squiggly stick in the mud that the tag attached to it assured would produce a bulbous candy-like fruit. There being no other choice, I reached for my mildewed shovel.

I did eventually get a Celeste tree which, when fully grown, has a rounded, inverted bowl shape, like a gigantic toadstool; a Kadota just reaches for the sky with no detectible pattern. My Celeste is still young, but I thought capable of providing some fruit by the next July. It did not. The Kadota, on the other hand, was a factory. Its fruit do not turn purple like the Celeste, so the discerning fig picker has to look for plumpness and grope for softness. Chomped into at the right moment the Kadota provides a burst of flavor that is, as expected, fig-like yet richer as though infused with nectar.

Now I am learning about other sprouts from the ground. On July Fourth afternoon, we stopped at a party where one of the guests was boasting about ice cream he had made from figs that grew in his backyard. What type of figs? Black Mission! "They grow plentiful," he said.

News Bulletin: It may be that local figdom has entered a new era. The once dominant Celeste no longer rules. Expanded plant nursery production around the country, rapid transportation and the new demands created by Katrina have opened the way for increased variety. The more choices, I guess, the better. Besides, maybe the Celeste will have something to give by Labor Day.

The Grapefruit and Me

This was the year I had to come to terms with what to do with too many grapefruit. The simple answer, I thought several years ago when I first planted the grapefruit bush, was to give them away. That, as I had already learned from the bananas that grew around the perimeter of the backyard, is not always so easy.

For all the talk about home gardening, the produce is not easy to dispose of, especially if there is the slightest blemish, as there likely is to be for something grown naturally without the benefit of some mad scientist applying genetic augmentation.

There have been some disappointments in backyard farming. The yard has yet to produce a meaningful fig crop. Last year, the satsuma bush underwent radical surgery to have a grafted stalk removed, but it did not survive. The kumquats are nice and sweet, but there are not many of them. And by my count, the yard has produced one lonely tangelo, made the lonelier since no one is really sure what a tangelo is.

There has been one success story though: the grapefruit bush.

Eating grapefruit is sort of like taking a long walk, everyone knows it is supposed to be good for you but not everyone feels like doing it, at least not today—maybe tomorrow. I will concede that the traditional method of eating a halved grapefruit, even with the serrated edge grapefruit spoon I ordered off the internet, gets a bit tedious. Seldom are the slices successfully lifted onto the spoon, more often is a miscellaneous squirt targeting the shirt that was meant to be worn that day.

Yet, my bush in the backyard is a beautiful machine, providing perhaps a couple hundred beautiful yellow grapefruit, many larger than the size of a softball. These, the Louisiana pink variety, have a flesh that provides a juice that is only slightly tart, yet sweet enough to drink.

I will gladly give a grapefruit to anyone who wants one, though I have become less of a pusher and more of a juicer.

That transition was not as easy as I thought. Most commercial juicing devices only have an opening for oranges or smaller fruit. Grapefruit-sized juicers are rare, so rare that I could not find one anywhere in the city. Though I tried hard to shop local, I admit to needing help from the web.

I am going to have to drink a lot of grapefruit juice to justify my investment in the juicer, but so far it is worth it. It makes a wonderful, slightly fibrous, juice, that when served chilled in the morning provides what has to be the healthiest breakfast juice of all. There are no additives, no colorings, no sweetener—just pure juice.

In my first year as a juice magnate, I have learned that it is better to make a half pitcher of the juice at a time, rather than a full pitcher, since, because there are no additives, the juice starts to get a little acidity after too many days in the pitcher.

Whatever its challenges, the one fulfilling fact about the proper grapefruit is that it grew in the backyard. It could even provide extra energy for starting the day with a walk—or maybe tomorrow.

The simple answer: drink up.

Limes can be made into juice too, only here there is more science involved. Only a rare person could drink straight lime juice, so there is more balancing off with water to dilute, and some sort of sweetener—not like the grapefruit which comes made to order.

None of this opportunity would have happened had Hurricane Katrina not knocked down the cypress tree. There is a lesson in there somewhere, but I am not sure what it is. Sometimes it is better to just experience the moment.

Moon Pies Over New Orleans

Moon Pies were not invented in New Orleans, but they should have been. The confection has a New Orleans quality to it—decadent and excessive. The marshmallow sandwiches are socially acceptable for tossing from carnival floats, and the logo of a smiling moon could also represent the Crescent City.

Though not of New Orleans, Moon Pies are of the South. They are made in Chattanooga by the Chattanooga Bakery. A subsidiary of the Mountain City Flour Mill, the bakery was created in the early 1900s to find a use for the excess flour churned out by the mill. According to the company history, through the years, the bakery developed nearly two hundred different sorts of confection items.

Moon Pies first rose over the Southern landscape in 1917. A true origin of the snack has never been documented, although one story traced the origin to Earl Mitchell Sr., an early salesman for the bakery. While servicing his accounts in Kentucky, Tennessee, and Virginia, Mitchell visited a company store that catered to coal miners. He asked what type of snack miners might like and was told that they wanted something that could be put in their lunch box and that was solid and filling. Mitchell used his hands to suggest a proper size. As fate had it, at that moment the moon was rising. One of the miners responded by using his hands to frame the moon in the distance. "About that big!" the miner supposedly answered.

Back at the bakery, Mitchell remembered the miners when he noticed some workers dipping graham crackers into marshmallow and laying them on the windowsills to harden. One idea led to another until a second graham cracker was added and the whole thing dipped in chocolate. The rounded moon-shaped snacks were given to company salesmen who offered samples along their routes. Response was enthusiastic. The new product was so successful that by the late 1950s the bakery was making nothing but Moon Pies.

Around that time, Moon Pies had been linked with another Southern product, Royal Crown Cola, a creation of the Union Bottling Works of Athens, Georgia. Moon Pie historians (and yes there are some) note that the phrase "RC Cola and Moon Pie" was once popular throughout the South, extolling an inexpensive snack combo.

Even cheaper is when the Moon Pies are caught off floats. Mobile pioneered the Moon Pie toss in its parade; now flying pies are becoming more common in the New Orleans Carnival.

Carnival also introduces the ideal accompaniment for the confection. Save the RC to mix with Southern Comfort; the way to toast Mardi Gras' closing hours is with a Moon Pie and champagne. Here the earthy, working-stiff qualities of the pie bows to the regal elegance of the bubbles as Carnival's kingdom embraces the Southern heartland and the cosmopolitan port.

Moon Pie marketers have done what they can to keep up with modern times. The pies now come in double decker size and in a variety of flavors. The cellophane wrapper announces the product as being, "The Only One on the Planet" and that the snack can be microwaved, though for no more than five to fifteen seconds. "Big Snack; Great Value" the wrapper also says though completely overlooking another virtue: the Moon Pie still fits nicely into miners' lunch boxes.

A Sandwich Named Drake

Whenever I eat something that I really like, I do not respond by saying, "quack, quack," nor, thankfully does anyone I know. Apparently, there must have been some sort of precedent for such a reaction by the late 1930s when a local company began making packaged sandwiches of the type that could be bought off the counter at convenience stores. The sandwich line was called "Mrs. Drake." The sandwiches were sold wrapped in cellophane with the two halves arranged side-by-side forming a triangle. At the top was a label with the image of a yellow Momma Drake duck, wearing a chef's hat, and four little drakelings at her side. An ad for the product included the line "quacking good sandwiches."

Philosophers and gastronomes alike have been vague on the subject of at what level of excellence is quacking good achieved. I grew up eating the sandwiches because I went to a grade school that did not have a cafeteria, but that sold Mrs. Drake products instead. Even at an early pre-acne age, I could talk with expertise about the choices. The tuna was the most tasteless; the Swiss cheese was too chewy (both existed primarily to appease Catholics who could not eat meat on Friday). Far more interesting was the luncheon meat and potato salad, though the salad was rather bland, certainly no threat to counteract the lonely thin meat slice. Leading the flavor list was the classic luncheon meat and pickle sandwich made with the meat slice and a spread that seemed to be a combination of mayonnaise and mustard. It was the pickle, though, that elevated the dish to its level of excellence. It was sweet and crunchy, delivering more bang to the mouth's gustatory cells than any other item on the counter.

Then came the big day.

Every so often there is a cosmic moment that tilts the world's spin, but in a good way, making the planet a better place to live. In New Orleans it happened the day that Mrs. Drake introduced a new and revolutionary sandwich, the "Li'l Barbecue."

Here the *chefs de cuisine* in the Mrs. Drake kitchen dared to be different. Instead of sliced bread they used buns. Inside was ladled with some sort of meat enhanced by some sort of barbecue sauce. (In retrospect I don't remember what type of meat it was. We kids didn't read labels much back then.) And then on top of the heap was—yes, it's true—a pickle slice just like in the luncheon meat sandwich and providing the same wonderment.

When the Li'l Barbecue was first introduced there probably was not much need to make the other sliced bread-based varieties (except on Fridays) because few would want anything else. Mother Drake had taken a new step and there was no turning back.

But then my life changed. When I went off to high school, I discovered that there were places with cafeterias that served hot gourmet dishes such as shepherd's pie and spaghetti with meat sauce. Life changed for the sandwich business too.

Convenience stores became fewer; fast food places became more plentiful. Mrs. Drake eventually disappeared from the counter, as would its traditional side dish, Dickey's Potato Chips, and its long-time nectar, Big Shot Cola—all locally made.

Maybe when something is "quacking good," that means that people will still be remembering it years later.

Boudin's Renaissance

An aunt in Avoyelles Parish traditionally would give me a pack of boudin for Christmas. It was a wonderful gift, except for the Christmas after Katrina when the car trunk tended to be loaded down with paraphernalia for survival in addition to holiday gifts. That following October I traced down the gamey, but still savory, smell that wafted from the back of my car to the Christmas boudin that had shifted into a space at the bottom of the truck. Guard your boudin well.

To most of the rest of the world, pigskin is that object tossed and kicked about during football games. That's true in Louisiana too, but the term has another meaning, also associated with the fall and winter, for that is the season of the *boucherie*.

Many churches and schools in French Louisiana are endowed by money from their fairs. On Sunday mornings, lines form to purchase the roast pig dinners made from the carcasses that glowed on vertical pits the night before.

Among the specialty items made from the hogs, the two most popular are cracklins and boudin. On paper, a cracklin does not seem like something one would want to take to a spa. It consists of deep-fried pork fat, with a hint of meat that is salted. When done right, though, there is a sweetness and crunchiness that cannot be denied.

There are two types of boudin; the red and the white. The former is the so-called blood sausage, and that is a discussion in itself. There are blood dishes throughout the world, including the English's blood pudding, but they are not for the squeamish.

White boudin is another matter. Pork, spices, and rice are mixed together and stuffed into a sausage case. Though it is an ancient food, boudin is thoroughly modern in that it can be frozen and then microwaved. Service hint: be sure to prick holes into the casing before heating, otherwise you might have a boudin bomb in your oven.

(Most daring of the variations are the boudin balls served from beneath hot lights at gas stations. That experience offers the extra advantage of being able to buy a lottery ticket while dining.)

Boudin and "kush-kush," a Cajun cereal made with cornmeal, are the subject of an only-in-Louisiana football cheer used at several universities: "Hot boudin, cold kush-kush, come on (name team), push, push, push."

In modern times boudin has gained popularity in the city. Once unheard of in New Orleans, it is now on the menu at some white tablecloth restaurants. At Jazz Fest, boudin in various forms, including crawfish, is sold.

Crawfish, of course, is not really a traditional boudin ingredient, but if the trend continues, that is perhaps good news for the pigs.

Presidents and Oysters

I wonder if the Secret Service frisked the oysters first.

When President George W. Bush once came to town. he dined in the Proteus room at Antoine's Restaurant where his meal included oysters Rockefeller. Now in these security conscience days, oysters are a pretty dicey food to serve a president, but whatever bacteria concerns that the oyster raises, they are certainly baked away in Antoine's ovens.

Bush's meal prompted a gleeful response from the Louisiana Oyster Task Force, a marketing group for the local mollusks which made a claim that might have otherwise escaped presidential biographers. According to the task force, Bush is a "longtime aficionado of Gulf oysters."

That information triggers a new untapped area of historical research: i.e., "the relationship between presidents and oysters." George Washington never came to the Gulf South, so he probably did not experience the local Gulf Coast oyster. He might have had the Atlantic coast kind, though probably without catsup and horseradish. The presidents from Massachusetts--Adams, father and son, plus Kennedy--all named John--were probably clam eaters. When it came to bivalves, the California presidents--Reagan and Nixon--may have had more access to abalone than to oysters. But neither clams nor abalone have the mass to be converted into classic baked dishes. Clams Rockefeller? It doesn't work.

Harry Truman was from Missouri where oysters are few, though as president he spent much time in Key West where he could have had oysters from the eastern end of the Gulf. And given oysters' rumored properties as an aphrodisiac, Bill Clinton might have had sacks of oysters sneaked though the back door of the White House.

My guess is that the presidents-to-be who had the most access to Gulf oysters were the ones who spent the most time in Louisiana. Zachary Taylor lived on a plantation in Louisiana for a while, so he could have had oysters in his dressing, and when Andrew Jackson celebrated his victory at the Battle of New Orleans, his victory meal reportedly included oyster gumbo.

Of all presidential oyster incidents, the one that should be noted and enshrined at the Smithsonian also occurred at Antoine's. It happened in 1936 when the eloquent Franklin Roosevelt was in town and was being escorted by the ineloquent Mayor of New Orleans, Robert Maestri. As the story goes, Maestri's handlers urged the mayor to speak to the president as little as possible so that his *yatty patois* would not clash with Roosevelt's high society diction. The mayor contained himself dutifully throughout the day but lost it when he gushed over the baked oysters that night. Turning to the President, he asked a question that has become a classic bit of local political lore: "How do ya' like dem ersters?" The president's answer was not recorded, though we would assume that he liked dem ersters real good.

Did Vice President Nelson Rockefeller ever have oysters Rockefeller? That may be lost to history. Also, since the Oyster Task Force claims that Louisiana harvests 250 million pounds of raw in-shell oysters per year, how many pounds are there when the oysters are taken out of the shell? Is anything left? President Bush was whisked away to a hotel after dinner; there he might have found time to add to his memoirs. Maybe some historian of the future will note a passage from that evening as the president revealed that he "really liked dem ersters."

DRINK

~~~~~~~~~~~~~~~~~~~~~~~~~~~~~~~~~~~~~~~

Roffignac—The Mayor
and the Cocktail

~~~~~~~~~~~~~~~~~~~~~~~~~~~~~~~~~~~~~~~

Compared to the guillotine, moving to Louisiana didn't seem to be such a bad choice. That was the plight of Count Louis Philippe Joseph de Roffignac, a native of Angoulême, France, who in 1766, was born with royal blood. His godfather and godmother were the reigning duke and duchess of Orleans. Their son would become King Louis Philippe.

Roffignac provides a compelling tale—a saga involving royalty, politics, booze, and maybe even conspiracy.

Being a royal might have brought some peer advantage when Louis Roffignac was growing up, but not so much by the 1790s when Frenchmen became preoccupied with revolution. In 1800, Spain had ceded Louisiana to

France. That was all Louis needed to hop the next boat to the new world.

Any guy whose godparents are nicknamed Orleans would have to be considered a fast social climber in a frontier town named after the family. That was the case with Louis, who became a state legislator, a bank director, and then mayor of New Orleans, a job he held for two uninterrupted terms from 1820-1828. He is remembered as being one of the city's best mayors.

During his administration, levees were extended, Royal and Orleans Streets were paved, and parts of downtown were, for the first time, illuminated with gas lamps. The city's first fire department was established, as was the beginning of a public school system. He raised money to plant trees, the forerunner of today's shady avenues. He also kept interesting company, having hosted both Andrew Jackson and the Marquis de Lafayette.

For all his accomplishments, however, Roffignac would also be remembered for two things. He was the city's last French-born mayor, but, most of all; a local alcoholic drink would carry his name.

Just how the Roffignac, the drink, came to be named after the former mayor is unclear, but the drink was on bar menus long after the mayor's time and into the era when the nightlife blazed with electric lights instead of lanterns.

Possibly the name traces back to there having been a brand of cognac named Roffignac made in the old country, just as Sazerac got its name from a French cognac (although that ingredient would eventually be factored out of the cocktail). Ok, here's the tricky part. There is a dispute, but in the end, I will resolve it. Early local-centric recipes were popularized by a Royal Street place called Mannissiers, which lasted from the late 1800s to 1914. In addition to its confections, the place liked to specialize in creative drinks long before the term "craft cocktail" came into use. Vintage Roffignac cocktail recipes combined cognac, some sort of raspberry flavoring along with simple syrup and seltzer.

Now here we experience an evolutionary moment: New Orleans, where barrel-laden boats drifted down from Kentucky and Tennessee, was a whiskey drinking town more so than it drank uppity cognac. Gradually it became common to replace the cognac with the upriver hooch. (The same thing would happen with Sazerac for which the namesake cognac would be replaced by rye whiskey.)

Served with ice in an Old Fashioned glass, the drink is a local version of the genre of slow slipping cocktails. In an age when the male work force spent many hours both during and after work propped against a bar, the Roffignac seemed to have its following. Gradually the drink was forgotten about, all except at Maylie's, the old Creole restaurant that lasted from 1876 through 1986. That the drink is remembered at all is probably because it was the house specialty there.

When Maylie's closed, so did the public life of the Roffignac. At some point, the whiskey would be replaced by brandy, and the raspberry syrup was swapped for one of several reddish ingredients with the most popular being grenadine, a mix made with pomegranate. Like music and foods, all drinks are fusion, shifting and adjusting with times. So at this stage in the evolutionary process, what can we say is the proper contemporary Roffignac? For this I defer to my friend Maureen Detweiler who has made it her mission to preserve the Roffignac, which she makes better than anyone has ever done. Her recipe:

Maureen's Roffignac
$1^1/_2$ ounces rye whiskey
$^1/_2$ ounce brandy
1 ounce grenadine
twist of lemon

Pour ingredients into an ice filled tumbler. Garnish with twist of lemon.

As for the former Mayor, his story should have had a happier ending, but it did not. Roffignac had returned to France after his stint as mayor, though with little joy. He reportedly complained to a friend from New Orleans that he regretted leaving the city. Perhaps it is better to be a former mayor in New Orleans then to be a former count in France. The circumstances of his death, at 80, in 1846 at his chateaux near Perigeueux, France, sound suspect to me, but here's the family version: One evening he was seated in an "invalid chair" examining a loaded pistol when he was suddenly seized by an apoplectic stroke and fell to the floor. The fall triggered the pistol, which sent a bullet into his head. He died instantly.

At the time of his death, Louis Philippe Joseph de Roffignac was said to be preparing for a return visit to New Orleans. It was a tragic end, but a good life: one worth lifting a toast either with raspberry or grenadine.

Sazerac: The City's Cocktail

1859 was an undistinguished moment of time in the city's history. It was two years after the first march of the Krewe of Comus, so the city's Carnival parading tradition was at least fledgling; unfortunately, it was only two years before the outbreak of the Civil War and the city, like the nation, would suffer from its impact. Barely noticed was the creation that year of a drink that would be identified as the city's classic cocktail, a reputation that would grow into the 2020s as the city's cocktail culture flourished.

To understand what happened in 1859, you have to first understand what was happening prior to that; New Orleans was going bonkers over imbibing. Folks here were talking about a concoction that a Royal Street pharmacist, A. A. Peychaud, had created. To a shot of brandy Peychaud had begun adding his family formula for bitters, a tonic compound that was offered as a cure for various maladies. The bitters, when added to the brandy, gave a kick to the drink.

In a city happy over brandy with bitters, next came John B. Schiller, a local agent for a French cognac importer who had an idea. The brand he imported was manufactured by the firm of Sazerac-de-Forge & Fils of Limoges, France. In 1859, Schiller opened a place on Exchange Alley in the French Quarter calling it the "Sazerac Coffeehouse." He was the exclusive purveyor of the Sazerac brand cognac (remember, cognac is a form of brandy), which he also served with bitters to create the world's first Sazerac cocktail.

Schiller had a hit on his hands, not that it took much to convince cocktail crazy New Orleans to try another drink. But as the city became more American and less French, tastes shifted. In 1870, Schiller's bookkeeper, Thomas Handy, bought the business and changed its name to the "Sazerac House." That's not all he changed. He kept the bitters but replaced the cognac with rye whiskey. As Stanley Clisby Arthur in his book, *Famous New Orleans Drinks and How to Mix 'Em* explained, the change was to "please the tastes of Americans who preferred 'redlikker' to any palefaced brandy." As the Sazerac was reinvented, no longer was its namesake, hooch, part of the recipe. Around that same time, Leon Lamothe, a bartender at Pina's Restaurant on Burgundy Street began adding a splash of absinthe (a licorice tasting liquor) to the drink. It became a standard ingredient.

Like boudin and bread pudding, the exact formula for preparing a Sazerac would differ from place to place, but Arthur's book codified an acceptable standardized list of ingredients:

1 lump sugar
2 drops Peychaud's Bitters
1 dash Angostura Bitters
1 jigger of rye whiskey
1 dash absinthe substitute
1 slice lemon peel

Most of the better bars and restaurants in town serve the drink that is best known as the house specialty at the Roosevelt's Sazerac Bar.

Peychaud's Bitters are now marketed commercially. The Sazerac name is also marketed on a brand of rye whiskey.

A Sazerac is my favorite mixed drink just because it is so authentically New Orleans and so authentically a cocktail. Like the city, the drink is a mixture of French and American influences. Even some of the ingredients—sugar and lemon—can come from Louisiana soil. And who knows, A. A. Peychaud could have been right, those bitters might just help cure most anything that ails us.

A Cocktail's Epic Journey

A very gracious lady seated next to the ice chest in the back of a bus made me an offer. She asked, as I understood her, if would I like "an old hen?" My reaction, I am afraid, was less gracious as I replied: "hunh?!"

I had been invited to take a field trip down the spine of Plaquemines Parish to the site of Fort St. Phillip. The date was March 3, 1999. Nearby was the location where in 1699, Iberville and his gang spent their first full day in Louisiana territory. As fate would have it, the date was Mardi Gras of that year. That coincidence would forever trigger the observation that from the moment that Frenchmen first arrived in the area it was Mardi Gras.

Back on the bus, I had a second pour of what I now understood was properly known as an Ojen (o-hin) Cocktail and not an ancient chicken at all. The drink, I would learn, originated in Spain, but New Orleans, and Rex, are critical to its survival. Perhaps because of early men's clubs, the drink would become popular with the Carnival set. It is the classic Carnival insider's cocktail. I would want to learn more:

Boatner Reily III was quite the man about town. The William B. Reily and Company Chairman had been a Carnival captain, had reigned as Rex, and was active in various other pastimes appropriate to uptown gentlemen. What brought me to his Garden District home later that year was a lesser known, but nevertheless important hobby of Reily's; he was part of a small group that had invested in buying a batch of Ojen from Spain. The anise-flavored liqueur was named after the town where it was made. Unfortunately, its market never expanded very much—except to one place on the globe—New Orleans.

To the distillery workers of Ojen, New Orleans must have been the epicenter of their existence. Here the drink was appreciated as a mixer for the main ingredient in an Ojen Cocktail.

Unfortunately, the product did not mix well with the economy. In the early 1990s the folks at Ojen said they were shutting down for good. Enter Cedric Martin, operator of Martin's Wine Cellar, who was a skilled first responder when the crisis was booze.

He bargained with the company to make one more batch, which he would buy. The company provided around five hundred cases, roughly eight thousand bottles, all headed to Martin's in New Orleans.

With that deal, and some help from his friends such as Reily, Martin became the world's purveyor of Ojen.

When I visited Reily, he had agreed to make his rendition of the Ojen Cocktail. With skilled hands he poured two ounces of the Ojen into a cocktail shaker, followed by a dash of Peychaud's Bitters, a splash of water and sugar.

There was one more ingredient, something that gets little attention, but this was going to be special: ice.

More later.

With the stash now sold out, Ojen was heading for obscurity once the remaining bottles were poured for the last time. But wait, Ojen has had a second savior—the Sazerac Company. The locally based purveyor of several brands, including the native Sazerac, acquired the rights to produce Ojen. (Owned by New Orleanian William Goldring, most of the company's products are produced at the company's Buffalo Trace Distillery in Kentucky as well as a few smaller satellite facilities.)

Which brings us back to Boater Reily putting the final touches on the drink. He pulled out a two-square-foot sheet of canvas. On it, he placed ice cubes. Then he folded the canvas to contain the ice. Next, he pulled out a small hammer and began pounding. Lesser men would have been content with ordinary crushed ice, but this was an act of urban pride. The canvas had come from the local Foster Awning company. Foster, besides being the namesake for the flaming banana dessert, provides the floor-wide canvas, with the crown in the center, used at the Rex ball.

Meanwhile Ojen has moved from near obscurity to legendary status with the opening of the Sazerac House Museum on Canal Street. The place does a brilliant job displaying the city's cocktail history including the Ojen, which is now home-based in a town once ruled by Spain and where the buildings in the French Quarter resemble those of Seville. The liqueur's odyssey continues—one sip at a time.

Oh, and as for the cocktail's other key ingredient, Peychaud's Bitters, Sazerac now makes that too. The ice you will have to get on your own.

HISTORY

How Bienville Got His Name

His name was Jean-Baptiste Le Moyne. His brother's name was Pierre. Because of the intricacies of 18th century French peerage and tradition, both would have extra words tagged to their name. Both would be more commonly known in history by names that had nothing to do with how they were baptized.

Landmarks in their honor, which would one day include parishes in Louisiana, streets in New Orleans and, in Pierre's case, a town in Mississippi, memorialize them with add-on ceremonial names, Sieur de Bienville and Sieur d'Iberville. Where did those names come from?

Due to the exploits and lineage of their father, Charles, the Montreal- based Le Moyne family had achieved French aristocratic status in Quebec. The French title of "*sieur*" is equivalent to "sir" in British aristocracy. As was the custom, nobility was often identified by land that they controlled. Dad Charles owned several pieces of land in France as well as Canada.

According to historian Micheline Giard, Sieur d'Iberville got his name "from a fief held by his father's family, near Dieppe, in the province of Normandy." Likewise, there is a village in Normandy known as Bienville from which Jean Baptiste got his name, though through a quirk.

"We do know that Jean-Baptiste assumed the title by default after the death of a sibling." According to Giard, "When his brother François, Sieur de Bienville, died in 1691, Jean-Baptiste received the landed title by which he would be known." (Just for fun, imagine if New Orleans was still a colony under the ancient French peerage system and a guy named Joe Smith would somehow inherit Bucktown, which did not exist back then, but play along. He would be known as Sir Joe Smith of Bucktown. That would distinguish him from other Joe Smiths and also establish the fact that he had land. With such a long name he might eventually be commonly referred to simply as "Bucktown.")

There are a couple of other curiosities about the founder's name. One is that the biblical character, John the Baptist (Jean Baptiste), is popular among the French. In the New World alone, there are two French Canadian cities named after St. John, one in New Brunswick and the other in Newfoundland. In the French Caribbean colony of Santo Domingo, a voodoo culture evolved for which the high holiday has been St. John's Eve. And in New Orleans the stream that the Indians called Choupithatcha was changed by the French to Bayou St. John. So, the city would be founded by a man whose given first name is very much in keeping with local French-based culture.

The other curiosity is the origin of the name "Bienville." It was common in France, as it is in Louisiana, to take the word "ville" meaning city and add a descriptive word to it. "Bien" in French means "good" so whoever first settled in the Normandy area thought enough of the place to call it "good city." Amazingly, the name would become the inheritance of a young explorer who would carry it to the New World where it would be attached to a town that in many wonderous ways is very much a *bien ville*.

The Truth About the French

Several years ago, I was at a breakfast where the then French ambassador to the United States was the center of attention. Over a selection of breads that certainly reflected frugality in the French entertainment budget, the ambassador received questions. Most were business-like queries about trade and commerce, but as the morning wore on and the ambassador wore out, I asked the question that had been bothering me most. "Mr. Ambassador, we Americans always hear that the French don't like us. Now, we're nice people. Why don't they like us?" He nodded. Being he was an ambassador, I expected a denial followed by a list of all the ways that France loves America. Instead, he gave an answer that was amazingly frank. "It is not the French who don't like Americans," he said, "it is the Parisians. But then the Parisians don't like anyone. My advice is to visit Paris in August when the Parisians are on vacation."

We all laughed. I paused to butter my croissant with what butter was left. Others in the crowd began to recite encounters where they found, if not love, at least acceptance in the old country.

Had that breakfast been today, I could have contributed more to the latter conversation because I have since visited a place where the French do love us— it is called Normandy. They love us for the invasion that liberated their country in 1944, and they love us for the invasion of American tourists, many descendants of the original invaders, who still walk the beaches. They love us every time they go to the bank, even if we are a little tiring in our uniform of Reeboks, football jerseys, and baseball caps. If that is the look of freedom, so be it.

Had the cheese not run out over breakfast, there might have been time to ponder how much Louisiana in turn owes to France, foremost for Louis XIV having sent Canadians to found a city. That not only defined us as a place on the map but gave us a carefree Latin character long before the more serious English or Dutch got here. And secondly for selling us. For the price of New Orleans, the fledging union of states got extra land thrown in stretching to Montana. Had the French not created a city on the big bend in the Mississippi River the British might have done so eventually, only instead of frolicking on Mardi Gras, we might be pouring syrup on Pancake Day.

While it still might be wise to avoid Parisians out of season, our cities share stories to tell. It was in that very building, the home of the French consul general, that a famous toast was exchanged during the 1960s. The reigning French ambassador was there that night to preside over what we assume was a more bountiful dinner. As the story goes, Vic Schiro, the then mayor of New Orleans rose to lift his glass. "I offer a toast," he said, "to the King of France." There was an embarrassed silence as the representative of a republic whose last monarch ended his reign at a guillotine rose to reply. "And I offer a toast to the Queen of America." Posterity does not recall Schiro's reaction, but there was reportedly good-natured laughing. A glass of champagne can always save a moment.

One Man's Wars

Like many other out of work Confederate officers, John Bell Hood came to New Orleans after the war hoping to find a future. The recent past had been tough. Early in the war, the Kentucky native had been regarded as one of the Confederacy's best commanders, but tragic defeats under his command at Atlanta and Franklin (near Nashville) had sullied his reputation. The war had taken a physical as well as a mental toll. He lost a leg and the use of one arm.

Other parts of him worked just fine though. In 1868 he met and (to her father's chagrin) married Anna Marie Hennen, a New Orleans woman of some wealth and special standing who was smitten to be marrying a general. Over the next decade, the couple had eleven children, including three sets of twins. They settled in a fine house that still stands on the corner of Camp and Third Street in the Garden District. Across the street lived the Mussons, a French family who counted the French Impressionist painter Edgar Degas as a relative.

There wasn't much need for soldiering in post-war New Orleans; indeed, native General P. G. T. Beauregard had gotten work heading up the local lottery. Hood became involved in a cotton brokerage and insurance business, had some early success but faced his own financial Appomattox in the winter of 1879, after a yellow fever epidemic forced the Cotton Exchange to close and depleted every insurance company in town. That summer there would be a smaller yellow fever outbreak that would take only eight people citywide. Unfortunately, three of the victims were in the Hood household, including his wife, oldest child, and then, on August 30, the general himself.

Originally the parent and child were buried in Lafayette Cemetery near the present site of Commander's Palace restaurant. Later the Hoods and three of their children were interred forever in the Hennen family tomb in Metairie Cemetery.

Left behind were certain legacies including the ten orphaned Hood children. What to do with them became a national cause headed up by General Beauregard. Failing to find a single family to take them all, the children were gradually dispersed to different homes across the country. Another legacy was the general's name. At his prime during the war, he headed the Confederacy's Texas Brigade. In what has to be perceived as an act of national benevolence, a US Army base in Texas was named after the general who once fought against the American flag. (The name though would not withstand cancel culture and has been changed to Fort Cavozos after Richard Cavozos, a Korea and Vietnam veteran who was the Army's first Hispanic four-star general.)

SEPTEMBER 2005. New Orleans was facing its worst crisis since the yellow fever outbreaks. Robert Hicks, an author specializing in novels based on the Civil War, is on a book tour to promote *Widow of the South*, a novel based on the battle of Franklin, Tennessee, where Hood faced a devastating defeat. By the time Hicks's tour reaches New Orleans, he sees a city in no mood for book signings. Instead, the author becomes transfixed with the city's post-Katrina plight and decides to do what authors do best, write another book.

Drawing from his knowledge of John Bell Hood, Hicks sees Katrina-like parallels of man vs. disaster. In Hicks's novel, Hood spends his last days trying to embellish his war record, in effect facing his own recovery. The book is called *A Separate Country* partially, Hicks explains, because the New Orleans experience was a separate country for Hood.

Hicks's work was certainly a novelty, a "Katrina-inspired" book set during Reconstruction and based on a Confederate general.

Then as now, New Orleans is a city of charm and challenges, one with possible battle lines behind every levee.

1927—A Year That Changed Louisiana

Several years ago, I sat down with my mom and one of her cousins to talk about the Great Flood of 1927. They were both little girls then, at a time of life when the adventures of a spring flooding disaster outshined the hardships created by it. The latter being for the grownups to worry about.

All along the state, the Mississippi River water, which had already been exceedingly high when pushed from the upriver states, spilled onto Louisiana soil. Much of it had been funneled through the connecting bayous and rivers, spreading equal flooding for all.

My relatives had lived in the Avoyelles Parish town of Bordelonville, where the water in usually placid Bayou des Glaises had been raised by the Atchafalaya River.

Family members had been evacuated to a Red Cross camp at Mansura, where the land is higher and where the girls could be wide-eyed with the experience of living in tents and where Red Cross workers handed out free Hershey bars.

Going home was not quite as much fun. In those days folks cooked with lard, which was stored in barrels near the kitchen. The high water had upended the containers and as it receded, left a coating of pig fat on the walls. To melt it off, a bucket brigade was formed, passing cans of hot water from a fire in the yard into the house where the containers were splashed on the already saturated walls. Flood insurance? FEMA? What were those?

Food was scarce. One of the few products that nature provided was crawfish, which had been driven from their burrowed holes in the ground. In those days, crawfish had not yet achieved their cult status and were regarded as a junk food; nevertheless, these hearty people of French, but not Cajun, ancestry gathered the critters and boiled them in salt, the only seasoning they had.

Ultimately, the flood would have an impact on the state's history, culture, and politics. A system of spillways was built to divert high river water. Many of the bayous were subdued by locks and dams (The once feral Bayou des Glaises was among many that were totally domesticated.). In 1974, Randy Newman recorded a song called "Louisiana 1927" telling about the flood's despair:

The river rose all day
The river rose all night

Something else significant happened in 1927 near the town of Marksville, probably not more than ten miles away from where my mom and family were encamped. A boychild was born. His name was Edwin Edwards. He would grow up seeing the hardships of rural Louisiana and hearing the passionate populist rhetoric of Huey Long who ran for governor in 1928. The flood would mold Edwards's politics, and the state's.

My Mom lived long enough to experience the state's other great natural disaster, Hurricane Katrina in 2005. That time there was no adventure and certainly no free Hershey bars. Her last experiences of the state were of it recovering, just as she saw it do after 1927. In between she had lived a good Louisiana life; knowing the fragrance of sweet potatoes in the oven, seeing the bayou banks in the spring when they are green and flowery, speaking with relatives in a unique Franglais dialect. She even developed an appreciation for crawfish boiled to be spicy.

Heavy rains occasionally force some of the state's small tributaries to flood, but the Mississippi River, contained by superior levees and flood gates has a beautiful presence; powerful, picturesque, yet, most of all—peaceful.

The Day Huey Long Was Shot

Joe Sabatier was a Tulane medical student, who in 1935 was assigned to work at Our Lady of the Lake Hospital in Baton Rouge "I'm not sure what my title was," Sabatier recalled, "but I think I was really an assistant to an orderly." The labor supply was inadequate, so medical students were pressed to do the work of orderlies, including the less desirable tasks such as inserting catheters in male patients. "But I learned how to do it," Sabatier added.

September 8 of that year would have been a slow forgettable Sunday until it became historic, as vehicles began to race from the State Capitol located on the opposite side of Capitol Lake to the emergency room.

Sabatier was off that day and had gone to the movies with a group of nurses. As the gang walked back, they noticed the speeding autos. "I went to my room," Sabatier recalled, "where I got a message to report to the hospital at once." Quickly the word spread. Huey Long had been shot.

At the time, Long was a United States senator who held a dangerous amount of control over the affairs of Louisiana. Through his handpicked governor, and with the support of many of his personally selected legislators, Long was the closest that an American state had ever experienced of a dictator. Throughout history, it has sometimes been the fate of dictators that when they could not be removed at the polls they were removed in other ways.

"When I got to the hospital they were preparing for the operation," Sabatier said. "I was told I was going to be a scrub nurse. Soon Long was wheeled into the room. "He was perfectly conscious."

Sabatier, who died in 2013 at the age of ninety-eight, may have been the longest survivor who was at the hospital that day when Long was shot. His memories include that of the long line of politicians who made their pilgrimage to see the wounded senator. Historians would later write that Long might have survived the bullet wound, except that the operation was bungled, and the attending surgeons overlooked that Long's colon had been pierced. "Later when people at the hospital began to talk," Sabatier remembered, "they generally concluded that he died of internal bleeding." Sabatier added that one of the senator's personal physicians was in New Orleans and in those days the road trip to Baton Rouge was still a slow one.

Long lingered for two days while cronies continued to line the halls of the hospital. He died September 10, 1935.

For all the commotion that the assassination brought to the hospital, Sabatier recalled that Long's funeral was an even bigger crisis. "Baton Rouge was so filled with people from all social strata," he said, "that the hospital was kept busy. Sabatier said that many funeral-goers, quite a few who were elderly, were brought in suffering from various conditions.

A native of Crowley, Sabatier went on to have a distinguished career as a physician spending a large part of his career in management at West Jefferson Hospital. He settled in New Orleans where he spent his retirement.

He was amazingly spry for his age and looked to be at least 25 years younger with a lean body and a head of hair that was not entirely gray. He had witnessed history and accumulated wisdom, including one major discovery: "I have done research, and I think I have learned the secret of longevity," he said. Then he whispered: "Selective choosing of your ancestry."

Not being a dictator helps too.

When Elvis Left the Building

Standing on the stage at Shreveport's legendary Municipal Auditorium, Winston Hall, a musician and tour guide with a passion for the city's music legacy, pointed to a spot on the floor, right up front in the center. The auditorium was empty that January afternoon, but the imagination quickly filled the seats as though it was Saturday night of yesteryear as radio station KWKH staged its weekly Louisiana Hayride broadcast.

Hall brought the moment to life by pushing the button on a cassette player which had a recording of a soundtrack from October 16, 1954. An announcer introduced a young man from Mississippi named Elvis Presley. After telling the crowd that he was proud to be there, Presley launched into a song called "That's Alright Momma." And then . . . from there on that spot on the stage . . . the music world changed. Really.

Because the concert was being broadcast, microphones were set up throughout the audience section. The sound technician quickly noticed that something different was happening. Teenagers, who had been dragged along by their parents to hear a country music show, suddenly seemed possessed. Turning the sound pods the technician integrated the screaming, unlike anything he had ever heard, into the song. Through the woods and hills of northcentral Louisiana and into Arkansas and east Texas the airwaves were raucous, as though sending a message that a king was born.

Louisiana, and New Orleans, would be part of the story:

Presley came to Louisiana often, most notably for the Hayride. For one of Elvis's Shreveport visits, the crowd was expected to be so large that the event was shifted to a larger facility on the nearby state fair site. The schedule was packed with mostly country stars. Elvis performed as the final act before intermission. His act left the largely teenage audience breathless and wanting more. While the show took its break, the audience began chanting loudly for Presley to return. There was so much commotion that Presley was snuck out through a back door where a car waited to whisk him away. But the crowd was still roaring. So, with what would become one of the historic pronouncements in rock and roll history, stage announcer Horace Lee Logan innocently spoke the now immortal words: "Elvis has left the building!"

Next to Huey Long's proclamation of "Every Man A King," no phrase spoken in Louisiana is as well known. Appropriately, Logan's message was about a man who by then was referred to as "the King."

New Orleans was also a frequent stop in Presley's career, including an extended stint to film *King Creole.* He would perform once on the big stage at Pontchartrain Beach Amusement Park. For that event, Presley was in the crowd of mostly country singers as part of a show put together by Red Smith, a local DJ for radio station WBOK (at the time a country station; later sold and switched to a soul format). The other big name was country singer Jim Reeves whose ballad "He'll Have to Go" would go platinum in 1960. (A not so big name was Anne Raye who that day had been crowned Miss Hillbilly Dumplin.)

Curiously the Shreveport Auditorium, which helped launch Elvis's career resembles very much our New Orleans Municipal Auditorium. Both opened at practically the same time; 1929 and 1930 respectively. The Shreveport building has lost none of its Art Deco good looks and still houses travelling road shows. Like any respectable old building, it is also haunted by ghost stories, though neither Hall nor a regular staffer who joined us claim to have ever seen an apparition there. (Although—there is a window that seems to keep reopening after being shut.)

Maybe it is the memories from the past hoping for a matinee.

On the Oswald Trail

"You're from New Orleans! You know who else is from there?" John our tour guide in Dallas asked, "Yes," I answered. To John the tour guide, New Orleans is a wonderful place to visit, but there is an asterisk. It is also the birthplace of Lee Harvey Oswald.

You can look at the fine museums, performance center, and nouveau modern buildings in Dallas; you can experience a bit of the quaint Texas lore in a downtown neighborhood called West End, where Stetsons and boots can be purchased at Wild Bill's Western Store or have dinner at the Y.O. Ranch Steakhouse where the menu includes rattle snake chili and buffalo filet. You can do all those things, but it is hard to ignore nearby Dealey Plaza and the sixth floor of the building on the corner overlooking Elm Street.

Our tour guide dutifully showed us the other attractions, but then as John turned a corner not far from a grassy knoll, the interest level increased as though flipped by a switch—this is what we were really there for.

Whenever there is talk about the events of November 22, 1963, there is always a mental asterisk. We have been conditioned to believe that there is still an unsolved conspiracy, even after a half-century's worth of global sleuthing. There is a lot to question, such as if any other evil force was behind the assassination, but there is one factor that is absolute, Lee Harvey Oswald did it—and he was acting alone from the Texas Book Depository. The murder weapon was his rifle. His past was that of a fanatic out to take his place in infamy.

By late 1963 the assassin-to-be was living in a one-story rooming house in Dallas's Oak Cliff neighborhood. John drove us to the place, which is now known as the Oswald Rooming House. Patricia Hall, the granddaughter of the woman who owned the building back then greeted us. At the time, sixteen men lived in the building scattered across different rooms. There was a common sitting room with a worn sofa and a black and white TV and a kitchen. The décor was basic Americana froufrou. "Let me show you Lee's room," she said. Had Oswald spent the rest of his life in a jail cell it would have seemed spacious compared to this tiny room that contained simply a bed, chest of drawers, and a chair. Here a twenty-four-year-old loner thought through killing the most important person in the world, who had lived all his life in spacious mansions.

After the assassination, and with Dallas in turmoil, Oswald returned briefly to the home that afternoon to get a jacket. (He had left his other one in the book depository.) That tiny room would provide his last moment of solitude. From there he began walking, with a pistol in his pocket, through the neighborhood. By then, the police were primed for a manhunt. We know the rest of the story: When a patrolling officer stopped the shooter, who no doubt looked suspicious, Oswald shot and killed him. He then ran into a nearby movie house where he was spotted, wrestled down, arrested, and taken to jail by a band of eager cops.

From that day, Patricia Hall's life was one of remembering Oswald, largely for tips. She was eleven at the time but claims to remember playing games with Oswald and some of the guys on the front lawn. Oswald would bring some notoriety to the neighborhood, but according to John, property values have generally stayed low. Neighborhoods of assassins are apparently soft on the market.

Not far away was another home where Oswald lived before his divorce from his Russian-born wife Marina. It was in the small backyard there that Oswald, dressed in black, posed for a picture, taken by Marina, showing him with a rifle and pistol and a copy of a newspaper called *The Militant.* This was the pose of a man with a mission. The picture would eventually become famous from being on the cover of *Life* magazine.

For Patricia Hall the case was still not totally closed. In the hours that followed the crime, she recalled, the FBI and other police rushed to the house. Her grandmother watched as they entered Oswald's room and carried away his possessions, as well as the towels and sheets. "They said they would return the sheets," she said, "but they never did."
Sometimes history suddenly changes directions.

Dale and Grace's Dramatic November

One November afternoon, Dale Houston and Grace Broussard stood outside the Dallas hotel where they and their group were staying. They were waiting for a motorcade to zoom by.

Grace was a native of Prairieville, Louisiana; Houston was born in Mississippi but spent a lot of time in Louisiana. Both were "rock-doo-wop" type singers with a touch of Louisiana Swamp Pop. Their talents had been overheard by Sam Montel, a record producer. He thought the two should join together and make a few records. So it happened that in September 1963 the two, to be known professionally as Dale and Grace, test recorded at Montel's studio in Baton Rouge, a few songs, including one that really caught the producer's attention. He sensed a hit.

In 1957, a California duo named Don and Dewey had recorded a soul version of that song called, "I'm Leaving It Up to You." The recording never had much traction, but Montel was aware of it and thought it might work for Dale and Grace. What came out of the speaker was a romantic ballad dealing with a couple in love but uncertain about their future. By 1963, a nation filled with post-war teenage baby boomers facing the same realities was listening. The slow dance song was what was referred to back then as a "belly rubber" adding to the emotion as the duo pined away:

> *I'm leaving' it all up to you. You decide what you're gonna do.*
> *Now do you want my love?*
> *Or are we through?...*

By October 1963, the song was climbing on the national charts. Dick Clark, the host of the national *American Bandstand* TV dance show and easily the most powerful entrepreneur of the genre, included the duo in his traveling Caravan of Stars.

And so it was that on this Friday morning, November 22, the caravan had moved into Dallas for a performance that evening. However, despite all the stars in the show, including teen wonders Bobby Vee and Jimmy Clanton, the biggest name in town was heading down the street in a limousine. For the moment, John Kennedy had achieved rock star status. Grace would recall waving at the president and thought that maybe he had waved to her.

Three blocks further down, as the presidential motorcade turned on to Elm Street and passed the Texas School Book Depository, the day; indeed, the world, suddenly changed. By night the nation had shut down, including the Caravan of Stars whose performances in Dallas, and then Oklahoma City, scheduled for the next night were cancelled.

Those shows would have been especially meaningful for Dale and Grace because that very week, their song had reached number one in the nation on the prestigious Billboard Magazine charts and had earned a gold record for selling over a million copies.

For a moment, before the tragedy, national greatness had intersected on Main Street in Dallas. There was the dashing young president and a couple from Louisiana whose song had moved the nation.

"I'm Leaving It Up to You" achieved a dubious immortality not only for its rapid rise to number one but also because it occupied that spot during the week of the assassination. As it happened, Dale and Grace were among the last people to see the president alive.

Like the couple in the song, a confused nation was asking what it was going to do.

The Beatles and Me

I achieved Beatle immortality on the day that the group played in New Orleans, Sept. 16, 1964. I'll admit that it is a rather shaky link to glory, and that it was appreciated by only one person who I did not even know. Nevertheless, given the improbability of my ever being associated with rock idols, I settled for what I could get.

My lunge to fame began that afternoon after I had returned from school. The whole town was buzzing about the Beatles who were performing that night at what was then called City Park Stadium. My cousin Marla had come in from Central Louisiana to be there. I was to be her escort.

She was more excited about the Beatles than I was. As a guy, I did not swoon over Paul McCartney's cuteness. I did not know about John Lennon's brilliance or George Harrison's zaniness, which really hadn't emerged yet. I might have been the only person going that night who was more interested in Ringo Starr, not because I knew much about his musicianship, but because I thought he had the coolest name ever. We American boys grew up with westerns. None of the heroes of the range had a name that seemed more appropriate for fighting outlaws than did Starr. Such a name should have been native to Dodge City rather than Liverpool. When the Earp brothers faced down the Clanton gang on the streets of Tombstone, someone named Ringo should have been at their side. Instead, Starr's fate was to be in the back rather than the forefront of his particular gang.

Though I was not likely to swoon, I was still interested in the cultural phenomenon, which was underscored that afternoon when the home phone rang. On the line was a girl who identified herself as a friend of a second cousin who had told her that my father worked for City Park. She asked if that was true. I confirmed that it was. That's when she became excited. She was actually talking to someone who was related by blood to a person who worked at the same place where the Beatles were going to be. "You must be the luckiest person in the world!" she gushed. At that moment my fame had reached its crescendo. I was her link to the Beatles.

That night, I could barely see the group perform. The stage was at the open end of the horseshoe-shaped stadium and there was no big screen TV. The real spectacle was the screaming girls who rushed the stage and the gallant police who tried to restrain them.

I never heard from the girl again. I was no doubt irrelevant to her by the end of the evening. Over time, the music from England would take its own course bouncing through posterity, like a rolling stone.

To this day, I think of the event as being less of a concert and more of a rodeo. Fittingly, keeping the beat was a guy named Ringo.

Beatles Rechanneled—Fifty Years Later

Elusive in the sky were diamonds. A dark canopy had blocked out the stars and from it a steady rain fell on those who had gathered at City Park's Tad Gormley Stadium to celebrate the fiftieth anniversary of the Beatles having performed there. A group with a legally proper name of the Fab Four and an uncanny ability to look and sound like the original band took stage and showed even greater power than expected. At the moment of the first strum from a guitar, the rain stopped, never to return. Umbrellas were closed; spectators now liberated from the weather had room to sway.

A half-century earlier, the Beatles were still a relatively new group with a limited repertoire. Ahead would be *Abbey Road,* "Sgt. Pepper," the mysterious *White Album,* evolution and "Revolution," and "Strawberry Fields Forever." This night, over a couple of hours, the Fab Four would perform the full Beatles repertoire. So in that sense, the show was better than what was performed on Sept. 16, 1964. Absent too were the teenage girls who stormed the stage and made the event more of a rodeo than a concert. Some were there, older by five decades, but still capable of conjuring up the excitement from that night. Paul worship never subsided.

Originally, the Beatles had planned to stay an extra day in New Orleans to meet some of the area's musicians. A last-minute addition of a performance in Kansas City changed all that. What a loss. Imagine if at some bar there had been a jam with the Beatles, Fats Domino, and Allen Toussaint. Might the muse have given birth to something great?

There was already a touch of local greatness in the audience at both the original concert and the recreation. Though the crowd was almost entirely

White at the time, by '64 this had changed so that he could cross the color line. His name was John Moore, and from the beginning, he was a big fan of the band from Liverpool. An aspiring musician, better known as Deacon John, he had been performing at local dances back then and still does today. The event's organizer, WYES-TV, saved a seat for him up front near the stage, where he could still be carried by the music:

> *Yesterday all my troubles seemed so far away.*
> *Now it looks like they are here to stay.*
> *Oh I believe in yesterday.*

A Fab Four performer who looked and sounded amazingly like the real thing sang "Yesterday" as the crowd swooned. Costume changes emphasized the many lives the group led, from the bright colored pop uniforms of Sgt. Pepper to the John Lennon lookalike dressed in denim and a military shirt lamenting the era's upheaval:

> *Imagine no possessions. I wonder if you can.*
> *No need for greed or hunger.*
> *A brotherhood of man.*

Another performer made up to look and sound uncannily like Ed Sullivan paced the show. It was Sullivan whose Sunday night variety broadcast gave the Beatles their first national exposure and who made the group famous. American TV launched the group's stardom; this night public TV was resurrecting the moment. There could be no denying though, the absolute genius that came out of Liverpool—music whose roots had been influenced by sounds coming from New Orleans.

By the time the show ended there were glimpses of stars in the sky. The storm that had earlier been ominous had in the end, cooled the night. Deacon John was beaming. The show had been great. Earlier that day, he had attended the funeral of Cosimo Matassa, the early producer of local rhythm and blues recording. Matassa's passing and the Beatles's one night resurrection bridged the transition in the rock and roll era. The music, in various forms, still brought happiness to its audience as long as they believed in yesterday.

Moon Landrieu and the Election That Changed Politics

One evening in 1969, New Orleans politics was about to change dramatically. At issue was the mayor's office. Back then, each political party had primaries to determine its candidate, but since nearly everyone in the city was registered as a Democrat, whoever won the Democratic primary would, in effect, be elected.

Televised debates were still popular then, ever since John Kennedy and Richard Nixon had starred in the first presidential debate in 1960. (The debate, it has been argued, gave the election to underdog Kennedy since he looked better on camera than did sweaty Nixon.)

By '69 TV debates were being used in practically every important election.

On stage that night were Moon Landrieu and Jimmy Fitzmorris. Both were council members-at-large; both had known each other for a long time; both claimed to be friends. There would be, however, one factor that, for many voters, would set the two apart: race.

Later in his career, Fitzmorris would recall in a newspaper interview that the election turned on a reporter's question during the televised debate. The question: "Would he promise to hire a Black man to head a major city department?" And his answer: "I said, 'No, I would not,'" Fitzmorris recalled saying. "I would not *promise* to hire a Black man, nor would I hire a Catholic, a Protestant, a Jew, or a Chinaman. I would hire the best qualified people regardless of race, creed, or color."

Fitzmorris's answer made sense in a good government sort of way, but politically it was a disaster compared to Landrieu's answer: He said "yes."

Fitzmorris did not mean for his answer to sound the way it did. He was responding to the word "promise" which meant that he wanted to keep the doors open to the best choices available, regardless of race. Landrieu on the other hand was on an ideological mission, there needed to be Black officials in city government.

Both Fitzmorris and Landrieu had won Black support in the past, but on this election, Landrieu would win an unheard of figure, more than 90 percent of the minority ballots.

There was also another factor. Something else had changed. In 1965 the federal Voting Rights Act passed. The law took away some of the rules, such as testing, that had kept some people from registering. With the change, the

Black voting numbers rapidly increased. In the past, Black political leadership depended heavily on the guidance of ministers. Among the heavyweights nationally were Martin Luther King and Ralph Abernathy. In New Orleans A. L. Davis and Avery Alexander were political/spiritual leaders. But after the Voting Rights Act passed, new groups, many organized by young men, emerged as a way of corralling the newly liberated votes. They had an alphabet full of acronym names including BOLD (Black Organization for Leadership Development), SOUL, COUP, and in the Treme neighborhood, TIPS. They became the new power brokers and were skilled at delivering the votes.

As Mayor, Landrieu gave the highest appointive position to Terrence Duvernay, a Black man from an old New Orleans family. Among the other newcomers was Sidney Barthelemy, who was appointed Director of the Welfare Department. Barthelemy would eventually be elected councilman-at-large and then serve two terms as mayor, a legacy of the Landrieu years.

Jimmy Fitzmorris would get involved in state politics and was twice elected lieutenant governor. In 1979 he ran for governor, but barely lost. Among those who endorsed him in his statewide elections was Moon Landrieu, and he would have strong Black support in New Orleans.

Politics was changing across the country, but in few places was it as identified with one man as in New Orleans with Landrieu. The sidewalks leading to Holy Name of Jesus Catholic Church on St. Charles Avenue were crowded for Landrieu's funeral on Saturday, September 10. The gathering included warriors from the Landrieu years now older but proud of the change they helped to bring about. On this day they were going to honor God and Moon.

Krauss—Character and Characters

What comes to mind first in remembering the former Krauss Department Store is the chimes. In the early days of such stores, there was a system of chimes with the number of rings designating some staff member. If, for example, the manager was needed there might be three chimes that would send him scurrying to the in-house phone system. Other personnel would have different combinations. At Krauss there must have been many issues behind the scenes because the chimes were like a symphony. Just during the time of a ride up the escalator there might be several signals, yet there was no apparent disorder. By the last days of Krauss, which closed in 1997, chimes were extinct in most department stores but not at Krauss, which rang the chimes as though striving for historic preservation. Another throwback was the credit system. In the days before everyone carried credit cards, a clerk would write up a charge slip. Then the slip would be put into a pneumatic tube system, sort of like what is still used at drive-through banks, to be whisked to some hidden away credit department from which would come the verdict whether or not to approve the sale. The system with its capsules whisked from floor to floor was both old fashioned yet somewhat jet age. It certainly had style, more so than waiting for a computer to approve a credit card.

Krauss was locally owned to the very end, and that in itself was unusual as other hometown department stores had succumbed to national operators. It had had a brief fling with having a suburban store at Lakeside Shopping Center, but that did not work out. (Here fate probably intervened because it should have been written that there should only be one Krauss Department Store.)

There were other quirks that added to its reputation; Krauss was known as *the* place for buying fabrics. Many dresses made for balls or proms were home-stitched on Krauss's cloth. The store also had an impressive collection of ladies' hats worthy of Easter Sunday or for promenades along Canal Street back when people still dressed to go downtown. The Krauss experience frequently included a stop at the lunch counter on the mezzanine where the food always had a good reputation, especially for a department store.

What really gave the place its historic legacy were some of its customers from the early days. The other Canal Street department stores were closer to the river, Krauss stood alone at Basin Street. It was the closest store, and this is important, to Storyville. Legends tell of the ladies of the red-light district shopping at Krauss for undies and other niceties. Many bordello-bound gentlemen, some having arrived at the former nearby train station, might have stopped there too for that extra embellishment.

Storyville closed in 1917, so Krauss was able to last eighty years without the red-light district business and just on its own quirkiness.

I once attended a cocktail party held on what is now the pool deck of a building now called the 1201 Canal Condominiums. It is the Krauss building having been converted to chichi living spaces. From the deck, I tried to envision the surrounding business district as it looked in Krauss's day: There was the Roosevelt Hotel in the distance; the Canal Line streetcars (then green rather than red); the skyline made jagged by bank towers and the river in the distance. Much has changed too; the old department stores Maison Blanche, Holmes, and Sears are gone, though their buildings are now hotels. Other buildings, like Krauss, are nests for condominium dwellers. That's not all bad. Having residents and not just day-trippers is good for the vitality of any downtown street. I do wish though that those who live there could somehow appreciate what Krauss was. It was a last of a kind whose character was suddenly whisked away—as though in a pneumatic tube.

When It Freezes

It froze so hard in New Orleans once that in order to shave, I had to warm the wash rag in the microwave. It was the Christmas freeze of 1989, a chill that blasted across from Texas, pulling a white sheet across Louisiana. Old houses, such as the one I was living in, don't take kindly to frigid winds that funnel beneath the raised floor, cracking pipes along the way. Having stopped the flow of heated water, the polar air allowed only an icy trickle from the spigot. It took the microwave several minutes to make heat from the dampened rag.

Freezes, really deep ones, are so rare that when they do happen, their impact is more keenly felt by a citizenry not used to them. During that same '89 freeze, city officials announced in midmorning that all workers should go home at once. Their declarations were poorly advised though, because they created the spectacle of a city full of sliding cars driven by people not used to steering on ice. Only the inevitable gridlock prevented more accidents.

Where there's ice there are some good moments too. By definition, the Schoen funeral home on Canal Street is not a happy place, but when the temperature slips below freezing, the fountain in front becomes a winter splendor. Draped with icy splashes, its stream stands petrified as though suspended in time. The fountain becomes a gauge to the temperature shift. When a trickle breaks through, that tells us that the weather has warmed a bit.

Once as a kid, some friends and I rejoiced in the first frozen tundra we had ever experienced. A January cold blast had frozen City Park's various ponds and puddles. Using old golf clubs as sticks and a block of wood as a puck, we glided in our shoes over an iced ditch playing makeshift hockey. Better yet was the layer of snow that we used to build a snowman atop a friend's car. He drove while another friend and I sat in a window on each side of the old Plymouth holding the snowman and waving to those along the way. "There was an unusual cold wave across the South today," the NBC news anchor reported that evening. As

WDSU, the New Orleans affiliate station, provided narration for scenes of Dixie under ice, there suddenly was the shot of two boys holding a snowman atop a car. My first and only snowman experience went national that night.

A freeze in New Orleans defies the city's semi-tropical character. For a moment, it's as though the town wears a new dress. Kids are thrilled at the changing weather; adults anticipate the plumbing bills. Dark coffee and chicory, warm and rich, and never really out of season, melts the chilled air with its aroma.

Old houses that were still blessed with floor furnaces were in their glory as people elbowed for the sensation of the heat climbing up their legs. Other old houses, still cursed with space heaters, were endangered by inflammable objects dangling too close to the flame and by the unventilated heater sucking oxygen from rooms made airtight because of the cold. Fire fighters stood on alert. These were the nights they lived for.

At some places, the homeless gathered as part of the city's "freeze plan"; at other places people happily gazed at the dancing, crackling flames in their home fireplace. The tropical nature of the city was blanketed for a few evenings but was never too far from bursting out.

Meanwhile there were the sounds—the roar of the chilled wind, the percolating of the coffee pot, the flutter from the fireplace and—the beeping from the microwave.

Edwin Edwards's Legacy Was No Joke

Accused of having taken an illegal campaign contribution, Edwin Edwards, who knew the law better than most judges, once offered a novel defense. For someone to have *made* the contribution was illegal he explained, however it was not illegal for him to *accept* it. Turns out he was right.

Speaking before an upstate group with evangelical leanings, Edwards was being goaded because of his reputation for womanizing. According to former secretary of state Jim Brown, who was there that night, Edwards turned the jeers to laughter as he explained, "I don't drink, and I don't smoke. Two out of three isn't bad."

When Edwards died in July 2021, the media and colleagues relished his one-liners. (Referring to David Treen, a Republican political opponent, Edwards once said, "It takes him an hour and a half to watch *60 Minutes*.")

At some point though, the conversation turned to the legitimate question about whether or not he was a good governor. Here too some might laugh, but on matters of governance he was to be taken seriously:

During his four terms as governor, Edwards was a builder, and he could bridge factions. Early in his first term he delivered a new constitution for the state, a task that had been a political quagmire. The document cleaned out many of the political obfuscations encoded in the earlier document and, in its day, was considered to be the model state constitution. In New Orleans when the 1984 World's Fair was stalled, he helped save it. He saved the Saints franchise from moving by cajoling Tom Benson into buying the team and persuading the legislature to fund improvements to the Superdome. He supported the deal to build the New Orleans Arena, which capped the dome's neighborhood as a sports entertainment area.

Edwards was born in 1927, the year of the Great Flood. That was also the year Huey Long was campaigning for the 1928 gubernatorial campaign. Long would dominate Louisiana politics during the years of Edwards's youth. Edwards was raised in the spirit of old-style populism. Government, because of its need to appeal to so many people, cannot always work perfectly, but if it gives the poor and needy basic services, that at least provides some hope for the future.

Edwards may have built too many hospitals, and he may have been too enamored with casinos, yet, just as Mussolini made the trains run on time, we see throughout history that the chutzpah that made scoundrels out of men frequently made them effective at moving mountains, or, in Louisiana's case, building bridges.

During the Katrina recovery, it was frequently lamented that Edwin Edwards, rather than Kathleen Blanco, was not in charge. (One difference is that supposedly Blanco was reluctant to accept President George W. Bush's offer to federalize the National Guard for the rescue. Edwards, on the other hand, confided to friends that he would have quickly allowed it. That way the federal government would have to assume more of the responsibility.)

In the famous gubernatorial runoff between Edwards and Klansman David Duke, a bizarre pro-Edwards bumper sticker proclaiming, "Vote for the Crook, it is Important" capsulized the public's perception of him. Edwards won with nearly 60 percent of the vote and left in the campaign's ashes one of his best one-liners by conceding that he and Duke did have something in common: "We are both wizards beneath the sheets."

Edwin Edwards's politics might not have always been delicate, but he produced results. He did ultimately get the federal government more involved in another way: US attorneys always had reason to watch closely whatever he was doing.

Election Night at the Monteleone

Working his way through the crowded ballroom, the old man approached the stage to which he had been invited. There was a problem though. So many people were offered a spot on the platform that wristbands had to be distributed. The old man had none. An official in the crowd who did not know who the man was had stopped him. He did not know that the old man through the decades had been on the stage at the Monteleone Hotel several times. Back then everyone knew who he was.

Moments later, the crowd in the hotel's La Nouvelle Orleans ballroom erupted with cheers as John Bel Edwards, who that evening had been elected governor of Louisiana, approached center stage, The governor elect thanked family and friends and told about how special the Monteleone had been in his personal history. In 1927, Bel Edwards told the crowd, his grandfather had run for sheriff of Tangipahoa Parish. On the afternoon of election day, he and his wife drove to New Orleans to stay in the Monteleone. The next morning, the new governor continued, "his grandfather bought a copy of the *Times-Picayune* to see if he had won."

Besides sanctioning a future governor's grandfather's election, there were many big stories in the *Times-Picayune* in 1927, the biggest being the Great Flood that devastated the state and flooded towns along the rivers and bayous. There was so much suffering that year that the mood was right for a populist who would promise to fix things for the little people. In 1927, little known Huey Long, a state public service commissioner, was plotting his gubernatorial campaign, which would lead to his election in 1928.

Long would tax the oil industries and build a state government that provided free services. His innovations included what would be known as the Charity Hospital system, a model for state-run free care. Among those that the new governor thanked that night was his mom, who had been a "Charity Hospital nurse who taught us all about compassion for our fellow human beings."

Also in 1927, in the town of Marksville, a future governor was born. His name was Edwin Edwards, and he would be raised in the formative years of Huey Long's populism. Edwards would be elected four times, more than any other governor. He was a bit of a scoundrel and very much of an achiever. All of his election nights were spent at the Monteleone. It did not take long for someone to recognize Edwin Edwards as the guest without the wristband, and he was quickly escorted to the stage. Though he and the new governor shared the same last name, they were not related. Their common bond was in being Democrats in a land of Republicans. For the former governor, the night presented one more opportunity to share in the hurrah from the stage at the Monteleone.

During Edwin Edwards's day his election night suite was number1450. This night it belonged to John Bel Edwards, though rest would be slow in coming. By 3:00 a.m. the victor was ready to retire, but some West Point buddies reminded him of a promise he had to keep. JBE and pals went to the hotel's rooftop terrace where they smoked cigars to celebrate the evening. According to a story by Tyler Bridges of the *New Orleans Advocate,* they were there until nearly 4:00 a.m.

One can only imagine what it must have been like that moment, to have just won a long-shot election and to be governor-elect. Below, the noises from the French Quarter, even at this late hour, could still be heard. In the distance were the skyline and the lights from bridges. Nearby is the Mississippi River that flooded in '27, but that is now tamed so that it can better channel the nation's commerce. Downriver was the site where Andy Jackson defeated the British. Standing guard over it all is the magnificent steeple of the St. Louis Cathedral.

Between puffs, the governor-elect might have sensed the history that surrounded him. Now he was part of it.

PEOPLE

Tennessee Williams Stories

Gore Vidal went to visit Tennessee Williams one day and saw him, thinking hard, sitting behind a keyboard. Asked by the author what he was working on, Williams responded, "*Streetcar...*"

Vidal was astonished. By that time, *Streetcar Named Desire* was already an established work having run on Broadway and won a Pulitzer Prize. It had become a classic American play. When asked to explain Williams answered, "I just don't think I got the ending quite right."

That story, as paraphrased by Professor Robert Bray, a Williams Scholar, was one of many heard at the annual Tennessee Williams and New Orleans Literary Festival. Bray added that Williams was always great with characters and plot development but worried about the endings.

Some of the stories are dark, complex, and censorable as was Williams' life. Other stories are pure whimsy. One of my favorites came from an early festival when a friend of Williams recalled that one of the playwright's favorite vacation spots, and later place to live, was Key West. On one visit, when checking out of a guesthouse he was given the bill for the stay. Williams said he was low on cash and asked if he could give a check. The owner agreed. The author filled it out, knowing that many people, especially in Key West, would not cash a check signed by Williams but save it as a keepsake.

Talk show host Dick Cavett, upon hearing the story, relayed that in the era before credit cards, cash strapped celebrities commonly pulled the same stunt hoping for similar results.

(A quick Cavett story: As a young man, on a warm day in Manhattan he first met Groucho Marx, with whom he would eventually become friends. Cavett approached the comedian saying that he was a big fan. "If it gets any hotter," Marx replied, "I am going to need a big fan myself.")

Cavett had many Williams stories, including one from when he came to New Orleans to interview, for his talk show, the playwright in the courtyard of the Maison de Ville Hotel. As part of the production, someone thought it would be a good idea to hire a carriage and have the crew ride along as Williams explained the French Quarter. It turned out the writer was more enamored by the neighborhood's fantasy than its facts. When asked to tell about a historic home called Madame John's Legacy, Williams responded that he had never met her; when prompted to talk about the Old US Mint, Williams answered that he had always wondered what went on in the building.

What went on in Williams' mind would have been the most bizarre tour filled with passion, despair, dashes of humor and gifted language. Ultimately his endings probably did not matter as much as the route taken to get to them.

Dinner With Tennessee's Brother

Being invited to have dinner with Tennessee Williams's brother would ordinarily be considered to be a great honor and it was. Only, anyone who knew Dakin Williams knew that with him, things could be different. Dakin was an annual visitor to the Tennessee Williams and New Orleans Literary Festival. He was not a shy man. The semi-retired St. Louis lawyer often wore a gold jacket with loud colored pants and always traveled with an entourage since he was convinced there was a conspiracy to kill him. Theatrically, he had been known to recite lines from his brother's plays including occasionally wearing a woman's slip when reciting as Blanche.

Dakin Williams believed until the day he died that his brother, about whom the New York City Coroner had ruled accidental choking from inhaling a medicine cap as the cause of death, had actually been murdered as part of some sort of back-stage intrigue to control his estate. Subsequent investigations never supported Dakin's contention, but he persisted. And that is why, he believed, he was a target.

Had there been a killer on the loose, Dakin's entourage could not have done much to stop him. At various times his group consisted of his wife who was a feeble woman; his adopted daughter, an attractive lady who drew lots of attention; a former cop who was also his driver; a young man with long brown hair whose role in the entourage was unclear but who was totally passive, and another man, we'll call him Charley, who offered no physical protection but had great stories to tell.

Among Charley's tales were that of his father whose insurance business in Memphis specialized in the needs of rhythm and blues performers. One of his clients was Elvis. Because of Presley's stature, his dad would open his office on Sundays to deal with the performers' needs while sparing the King the inevitable groveling from a waiting room crowd. Charley, who was a kid, would go to the office with his dad. Elvis would get restless while the older man was processing forms, so to pass time he would wrestle on the lawn with Charley. They became friends, and Elvis would invite Charley to parties at Graceland. Eventually Charley stopped going, he lamented to me, as drugs became more a part of the scene.

Oh, for simple days of just wrestling with Elvis.

Dakin was a man of some wealth and his dinners, always held at an upper-end French Quarter restaurant, were lavish affairs where food and booze flowed. The honor of being there was tempered only by Dakin's tendency to, on the days of the dinner, invite just about anyone who he met that day providing they were not trying to shoot him. On this particular night, Dakin had returned from an afternoon at Harrah's. The expanded guest list included the members of a band performing at the casino. There must have been a total of about twenty guests, a few of whom might have actually heard of Tennessee Williams.

So, I sat at the end of the table opposite Dakin and heard stories from Charley about Elvis. Dakin's wife tried to be gracious despite this really not being her type of crowd. Meanwhile, a local attorney who was ogling Dakin's daughter had gotten himself invited and continued his pursuit. The kid with the long hair ate quietly. The band members gobbled up the grub. The setting could have provided characters for a play.

Dakin was in his glory. He lived in the shadow of his brother but always cast his own light.

Allen Toussaint at the Keyboard

Several years ago, at Jazz Fest time, I was working on an article about New Orleans musicianship, especially piano playing technique. I needed badly to talk to an expert and figured I could do no better than to get Allen Toussaint, the city's famed song writer, on the phone.

There were two surprises. One, somehow, I actually got hold of his number; and two, he answered. For a man of his stature in the music industry, I was braced for the call to be blown off as another inquiry from a music geek but no, and this was surprise three, he actually embraced the topic. Piano playing was his life; what he wanted to talk about. He was cordial and tried his best to make sense out of a complex question. The conversation needed embellishment. That's when he paused to offer instrumental examples. I had not realized it, but the whole time we had been talking Toussaint was sitting at a piano. He was in his natural environment as he placed the receiver to the side and began to play different examples of New Orleans style.

This was a motherlode. Forget about the interview, I was having a private concert, enriched by explanations, from Allen Toussaint. I learned something about New Orleans piano music from the experience, and a whole lot about Allen Toussaint, who was as classy as he was prolific and creative.

His profile of song hits; most written for others, some performed by him, included:

"All These Things"
"A Certain Girl"
"Fortune Teller"
"Holy Cow"
"It's Raining"
"Lipstick Traces"
"Mother-in-Law"
"Southern Nights"

"Whipped Cream"
"Working in the Coal Mine"

All of these songs create sweet memories for somebody; some romantic some humorous, such as singer Benny Spellman's bass refrain of "Mother-in-Law" dispersed between Ernie K-Doe's lyrics about domestic frustration.

"Southern Nights," which Glenn Campbell recorded, could have been made into poetry recalling warm evenings beneath stormy skies. While performing that song, Toussaint would drift into a recitation of youthful memories that was theater in itself.

Toussaint died suddenly November 10, 2015, at seventy-seven, during a trip to Spain. Like everyone else who knew of him, I wish I had had a chance to hear him more often. I do remember my last memory and it was certainly an expression of his generosity:

In June 2012 the city was abuzz about the plans of the Newhouse chain to reduce publication of the *Times-Picayune* newspaper to three times a week. Besides the loss of news coverage, many of the publication's employees were losing their job. A rally was held at the parking lot of Rock'n'Bowl to help support the newly unemployed. Toussaint is a big star who could have commanded huge fees. This day he was a volunteer performing at a keyboard on a makeshift stage.

"Allen Toussaint has rescued the careers of many singers," I would write, "but I never thought he would be needed to help salvage the *Times-Picayune*. There he was though, in the Rock'n'Bowl parking lot performing at a rally to save the newspaper from marginalization at the hands of its owners.

"Toussaint's opening song, 'Holy Cow,' one of his many classics, summed up the situation perfectly, as though written for the Newhouse clan and their accomplices:

> I can't eat.
> And I can't sleep.
> Since you walked out on me, yeah.

"'What's going on?' a truck driver who was paused at a stop sign asked as I waited to cross South Carrollton to attend the event. 'Is there free music or something?' I explained that it was a rally to try to save the newspaper. 'Oh yeah,' he responded, 'that three times a week thing, that ain't no good.' Then he drove away."

In January 2022, what was Robert E. Lee Boulevard was renamed Allen Toussaint Boulevard. There was never any real disagreement about Toussaint's worthiness to have a street named after him, though there was at least one suggested alternative—Gentilly Boulevard. Toussaint lived in that neighborhood, plus at one point the street parallels the Fair Grounds where the Jazz Fest is held.

In terms of New Orleans musical legacy, however, all roads somehow connected through Toussaint.

Dave Dixon and the Making of the Saints

Dave Dixon would break out in a laugh every time he told the story that happened in 1966. Dixon, who died in 2010, lived a life with plenty of reasons to smile, including being able to witness the Saints' Superbowl win. At some point there needed to be an ovation for Dixon, the antiques dealer turned civic activist. Without his tenacity all those years ago, there would be no Superdome; without the dome, New Orleans would have never been given an NFL team. Without Dixon, this city would be a mere "Who Dat" whenever the topic is professional football.

Dixon had plenty of stories to tell on the way to his favorite one. There was the time, for instance, he had to convince the NFL lords that New Orleans was interested in professional football. With the support of George Halas, the then owner of the Chicago Bears, a rare pre-season doubleheader was played at Tulane Stadium. One problem though, was that Louisiana law still required public gathering places to be segregated by race, but the NFL would not permit that, and the Tulane Board, which allowed use of the stadium, was also anxious to see the law ignored.

An announcement was made publicly that tickets would be sold on a first come, first served basis. To a surprised Black population, that translated into being able to sit wherever they wanted. There was no problem at all from the racially mixed seating Dixon recalls, but then a heavy rain drove all the fans into the dry areas beneath the stands. Dixon remembers hearing a great uproar from the compact, rain-drenched crowd. He hurried to the area fearing racial tension. Instead, he found a party. Everybody was just eating and drinking and having a good time, Dixon says, then when the rain stopped, they went back to the game. "I was also worried about the teams," Dixon remembers, but "Halas told me, Dave, the Chicago Bears will stay here until 4:00 a.m. if they need to."

In 1966, New Orleans was awarded an NFL franchise. Passage of the federal civil rights laws had in effect opened the South. A year earlier Atlanta had been given a team. New Orleans won because of its enthusiasm, its charm, but mostly because of the help that the NFL got from the state's then-powerful congressional delegation. The league needed help fending off anti-trust laws as it sought a merger with the rival American Football League. None of that would have happened though without the maneuvering of Dixon.

When Commissioner Pete Rozelle called to tell Dixon that the NFL was coming to New Orleans, it was Dixon who suggested that the announcement be made on November 1, All Saints Day. At the time the team did not have a name, or an owner, but Dixon pushed hard for the name "Saints." Why? "Because I knew it would be free publicity every time the song was played."

A local law firm urged one of its Houston customers to apply for ownership. Eventually the league accepted the application of the oil-rich Mecom family to own the team. Poppa Mecom put his twenty-eight-year-old son, John, in charge. Dixon admits that at first, he did not like young John Mecom because of his playboy image, but it was the new owner who would have the final say over the team's identity.

And that leads to Dixon's favorite story: Mecom began to have second thoughts about the name. One evening a Mecom aide had dinner with Dixon to explain that his boss was concerned that the name might seem sacrilegious. Dixon would recall the moment with glee. Philip Hannan, the archbishop of New Orleans, happened to be in the restaurant. Dixon apologetically interrupted the archbishop and posed the question. Would calling the team Saints be sacrilegious? "No," the bishop answered, "besides I have a premonition that this team is going to need all the help it can get."

At that moment, as though baptized by the bishop, the New Orleans Saints came into being. Hannan was right. The team would have some tough times in pursuit of glory, though it has always been blessed by the vision of Dave Dixon.

We pray, however, that there is a statute of limitations on the bishop's premonition and that there are more super events in the team's near future.

Al Scramuzza at 1826 North Broad

Sometimes the greatness of an individual can be measured by the poetry of his words. Consider these three quotes on the subject of winning:

"Nothing can seem foul to those that win."   —William Shakespeare

"Victory at all costs, victory in spite of all terror, victory however long and hard the road may be; for without victory, there is no survival."
                                                                                        —Winston Churchill

"Stay with Al Scramuzza and you'll never be a looza."   —Al Scramuzza

What can be said of a state that created Edwin Edwards, Tom Benson, and Al Scramuzza in the same year, 1927? 1927 also produced the Great Flood, which, come to think about it, is also part of the story, more later.

Edwards, Benson, Scramuzza—a triumvirate in which each member can claim great accomplishments; for Edwards the current state constitution; Benson has a Super Bowl ring, and Scramuzza, by his account, made the crawfish popular,

Once regarded as a junk food, the little red critters did not begin achieving widespread consumer recognition until the 1950s when Scramuzza began selling them. Such a conversion of tastes required marketing, and here Scramuzza was a master. By the 1980s, he was starring in a series of seafood commercials, some of them showing him dressed as a doctor playfully proclaiming that crawfish was good for just about all that ails a person—a fact that even the great Dr. Ochsner apparently missed. While he delivered his message, the chorus sang those memorable words, "Seafood City, very pretty," touching on the fundamental truth that customers expect beauty from seafood joints. Lest there should be any doubt where Scramuzza's store, Seafood City, stood, New Orleanians were infected with singing the jingle's punch line, "1826 North Broad!!"

Added to the appeal was that Scramuzza had a look, featuring a pencil thin moustache beneath a prominent proboscis, and a name that was made for merriment. Edwin Edwards spent much of his career facing voters and jurors; Benson dealt with bankers and team owners; Scramuzza—he faced the mighty tide of those with a craving to suck heads.

Now back to 1927: Many Louisianans were sent to Red Cross relief camps that year as they waited for the water to recede. The story that has been handed down by relatives is that when their kinsmen returned to their farms in central Louisiana, they were dismayed to see that the water had driven crawfish all over their lawn. They were poor people; nevertheless, this was a food that they did not eat, but these were hardly times for being picky. The wild crawfish were plopped in pots, seasoned with salt, and boiled until they turned red. It was the plight of refugees to have crawfish boils forced on them,

Even in hard times, they were never loozas.

Meyer the Hatter: Life on Top

Several years ago, my wardrobe for spending an afternoon at the French Quarter Fest included a spiffy new panama hat. Somewhere along the Riverfront, a fellow fest-goer stopped me and said, "nice hat." With local pride I replied, "I got it at Meyer the Hatter." "I know," the man answered, "I am Meyer."

He sure was. In an age when small businesses have disappeared as though flooded by the Amazon, Meyer the Hatter's store has survived.

There are two things that the shop, located at 120 St. Charles, right off of Canal Street, has plenty of; one is hats. They are all over: in the display windows, on the counters, on shelves; behind the counters; on people's heads and stored in two upstairs floors.

And the other plentiful fixture is people named Meyer. They too are everywhere: brothers, sons, a wife, a daughter-in-law, cousins, whatever. Sam Meyer himself is third generation, having followed behind his grandfather, Sam H. Meyer, who founded the store in 1894 and Sam's father, Andrew, who started selling hats there in the 1920s. Sam II tossed his hat into the ring, so to speak, in the 1940s. He and his late brother William brought the store into the future, including moving to the current location. It takes lots of room to claim the title "The South's Largest Hat Store."

I have a special fondness for the block, more so for what it was than what it is. In the days when the downtown workforce was practically all male, this was the most masculine of blocks. There was the hatter plus Pokorny, selling men's shoes, Rubenstein's Men's Clothes, and a men's luncheon club. Across the street was Kolb's, serving those heavy masculine German foods, and then there was the Pearl, an oyster spot whose fare included the very masculine past time of downing a "dozen raws" on the half-shell. Meyer adapted his hat selection to serve needs of all types, such as those white caps that jazz musicians wear or top hats for the ball.

I was there to cash in on a gift certificate. My selection was a gray all felt hat, with a clump of feathers stuck in the hat band on the left side. The wide brim gave the hat an Australian look, though without the prerequisite to fight a crocodile. Inside was a white card with the totally classic Meyer message: "Like Hell It's Yours. This hat belongs to _____. But you can get one like it from Meyer the Hatter." Thusly are hat thieves scared away.

Meyer himself was wearing a red hat while he worked the floor. Keeping up with modern times, he gave me a koozie displaying the store's latest slogan, "Love your Hattitude." A customer had suggested it to him. One with hattitude.

Now I digress for a finale with a sad ending. Back to the panama hat that the hatter had spotted me wearing. I like trains, and later that year we took a trip to Chicago and back. On the last leg of the ride, as the train approached New Orleans, I was packing and I could not find the hat. The sleeper rooms are so small that it is hard to lose anything, but there was no hat. I asked the attendant if maybe he had placed it somewhere. He hadn't. Just to be sure though, he pulled down the overhead bunk which is pushed up to ceiling level during the day. There it was. The attendant had not noticed the hat on the bed. Now it was a smashed disc of straw.

Life continues; the trains keep rolling. There was some irony though that the hat met its demise on a train called the Panama Limited.

Harold Judell: Secrets and Solutions

Harold Judell never revealed the end of the story, but the beginning was certainly intriguing. At the time of the outbreak of World War II he worked for the FBI in Washington, where he was a go-to guy for J. Edgar Hoover. Since there was no CIA at the time, the FBI handled foreign matters, so Judell was sent to South America. Allied intelligence had received word that the Japanese had set up a command post in Peru. Such a presence would have given the enemy a foothold to overseeing activity in the Eastern Pacific as well as throughout the continent. The center of the espionage had been pinpointed to a Japanese laundry in Lima. Judell was part of a group sent to visit the laundry.

What happened next? We do know that the visitors were not there to get their shirts cleaned. All that Judell would concede was that by the end of the day there was no more Japanese laundry. In 2006, on the occasion of a significant birthday, I tried hard to break the story. "Harold you're ninety now, the war has been over for sixty-one years, can you tell now what happened at the laundry?" "No," he answered with the determination of a guard at Fort Knox.

Later in the war he was stationed on the Dutch island of Curacao. Word had been received that there were Japanese submarines in the area with the intent of opening fire on a refinery at the far end of the island. Judell contacted the

US Navy to see if planes could be sent to attack the subs, but the word came back that there was no aircraft in the area. The island would have to suffer the consequences. Later that afternoon, Judell sat with the governor general on his veranda, each with a tropical drink, as they watched the firework-like show of explosives in the distance.

Judell would also have a colorful post-war career. The Milwaukee native eventually settled in New Orleans, where he had earned a law degree at Tulane, and became a prominent bond attorney. The work got him involved with politicians, and the list stretched far. Imagine in one lifetime having worked alongside Hoover and Earl Long.

During the 1960s when the state was studying the possibilities of building a domed stadium, there was one huge obstacle, how to pay for it. Moon Landrieu, at the time a city councilman and a member of the dome commission, recalls talking to then-governor John McKeithen and the two were stymied about raising funds. They decided to call Judell. It was he who developed the bond-financing plan that made the dome possible. "Without Harold," Landrieu would tell the *Times-Picayune*, "I don't think it would been done."

I personally witnessed a less visible, but crucial in its own way, moment when Judell had been appointed to a "blue ribbon committee" to resolve a volatile Carnival discrimination ordinance that had been proposed by a city council member. The issue divided the city socially and racially. Judell worked quietly to bring about a compromise. Finally, an acceptable plan was brought before the entire committee. The mood was good. Approval was imminent, but at the last minute someone questioned one line of the document that could have been misinterpreted. There was concern. The whole issue was about to explode again. But then Judell approached the document, pulled out his fountain pen, scratched out the questionable sentence and replaced it with the sort of legalese that only an experienced lawyer would know. Everyone approved. The document passed unanimously.

Business was good and he became wealthy. At one time, he owned a French Quarter hotel as well as a St. Charles Avenue apartment building, but the real gold in his life, that New Orleanians knew best, was his second wife, Celeste Seymour Judell. She was a strikingly attractive woman whose mother had been a silent movie era screen star. The couple spent much time in New Orleans when they were not traveling, quite often as spectators to major tennis tournaments, or at her condo in Manhattan. Celeste became a big supporter of the New Orleans Opera and public television. She exuded style and excellence. There was no more elegant couple whose lives had been such an adventure than Celeste and Harold.

Services for Harold Judell were at St. Patrick's Church, a place he had helped support. The aisles were filled with old friends and colleagues. To the end his life has been one of stories to tell, and secrets to keep.

An Elvi's Last Ride

At nearly 6:00 p.m. on Saturday, June 8, a crowd gathered at the edge of the old Treme neighborhood outside a fledgling distillery, where the locally made products included Gentilly Gin, Bywater Bourbon, and Marigny Moonshine. Many in the group were costumed, some as variations of Elvis. They were there to remember Macon Moore. Earlier, good spirits had flowed freely inside as tributes were made to the deceased.

Moore was a native of Richmond, Virginia, but really belonged in New Orleans where he eventually settled. By profession he was a hospital administrator; by passion he lived for Carnival. He belonged to several Carnival groups but would be best remembered as a founder of the Rolling Elvi, the group that thunders through parades with each member dressed as the King and riding a motorbike. (There is no obvious connection between Presley and the scooters. Some things, especially on matters of Carnival, just have to be accepted)

It happened that the gathering was at the corner of North Claiborne and Bienville; named after, respectively, the area's first American governor and the city's founder. And what a city they created. To a smattering of drum beats the crowd congregated behind a waiting brass band. Only in New Orleans are the departed remembered so sweetly. First there was the slow dirge as the band moved slowly and the crowd stepped carefully.

All of this was happening on a weekend when New Orleans experienced an uncanny showering of loss among those who carried the culture. Earlier that day, there had been a visitation for restaurateur Leah Chase. On the day before, bluesman Dr. John climbed the stage at voodoo heaven. Two weeks earlier, color writer Ronnie Virgets, who would have been in overdrive writing about all this, signed off.

Macon Moore had been more of a behind the scenes organizer, but it takes rare ability to, in the final act, pack a street with Elvises. The procession moved down along Bienville with the music building to that special moment when the mourning segues into cutting loose and the followers begin to dance. So too did the neighbors, one of whom, only moments before was sitting on the porch of his shotgun home drinking a beer and was suddenly transported to the sidewalk, jiving to "Little Liza Jane" while waving a beer can as his goblet.

As a city with so much culture, we always worry about losing it, especially as every second line steps down the old streets. If there is hope, it was in the faces of the band from Young Audiences of Louisiana, a charter school group, whose students were experiencing all the quirkiness from the street level.

No one knew it at the time, but just that day there had been yet another loss. Spencer Bohren, who specialized in blues and American roots music, left the spotlight due to cancer. Only three weeks earlier he had been interviewed at Jazz Fest. Like Moore, he too was from elsewhere, Wyoming, but would be captivated by New Orleans.

Making several right turns along the route, the procession returned to its starting spot stepping down North Claiborne back to the distillery whose nectar could help temporarily soothe the sorrow. For all the departed, the eternal question of the second line continues, "Didn't they ramble." To which the answer is always yes. This moment, though, belonged to Macon Moore.

Channeling James Booker

An aged poster located on the wall next to the piano proclaims, "BOOKER'S BACK BAR Piano Sessions." Next to those words is a drawing of a frail black man wearing a band musician's cap plus glasses and a t-shirt that says, "Maple Street Bar."

There was a day when this simple room located beyond the Maple Street's main stage echoed with some of the finest piano music in a city already known for its keyboard greatness. On many Thursday nights, fans would fill the room to hear James Booker who, some would say, was the city's best piano player ever.

Dr. John, the gravel voiced voodoo piano wizard who took organ lessons from the versatile keyboarder thought as much. In his gruff style, the Dr. affectionately called Booker "The best Black, gay, one-eyed junkie piano genius New Orleans has ever produced."

Harry Connick Jr. worshipped Booker from childhood through stardom. Connick would narrate a documentary about Booker called *Bayou Maharajah*. An article about the production quoted Connick breaking down Booker's style. "He shows the left hand doing one thing, the right hand doing another thing, and also finger by finger. With Booker, every finger was doing a different thing, referencing a different part of the song. It's incredible. It's unlike anything else before or since."

Booker's life was brilliant but tormented. His lost eye came from being hit by a speeding ambulance when he was ten years old. That, however, would contribute to his flamboyance. Many times, he wore a black eye patch with a bright star in the center, He would blame the trauma from the eye injury for his drifting into drugs. Heroin and alcohol were his devils leading to his eventually serving a year at Angola penitentiary and a month in parish prison.

Somehow, through it all, he mastered the keyboard. Those who knew music knew that Booker's talent was extra special, from a special city:

One Thursday night, Bill Malchow, a piano player from Connecticut who had lived in New Orleans before he and his wife moved to New York, revisited the Maple Leaf. In the Big Apple he has gathered many gigs, though no one else includes so many elements of New Orleans in their repertoire.

Because of the French Quarter Festival and the Jazz Fest, many expatriate musicians revisit home as though being lured back to Eden. During his visits, Malchow usually manages to have a night at the piano in Booker's Back Bar. For an hour and a half, his hands, like Booker's, glide the keyboard in full glory, mixing in blues, rock, funky stuff, and the classics.

James Booker was born in New Orleans on December 13, 1939 and spent some of his growing up years in Bay St. Louis. He died November 8, 1983 from, as one reviewer said, "hard living," related to heroin and alcohol.

His time sitting at a keyboard was his salvation and his gift to mortals. For a man who lived such a tormented life, one of Booker's greatest, and my favorite, performance pieces was "Sunny Side of the Street." Somewhere among the demons in his soul a chorus of angels sang too, especially as they performed the 1930s post-Depression classic that defied listeners to keep still or to not smile. A YouTube recorded version ends with a riff from Booker's other instrument, his voice, as he sings the audience into delirium.

Perhaps in deference to Booker, Malchow ended his set last Thursday with another song about happiness, "When You're Smiling," a 1928 classic recorded by many including, like Booker, another New Orleanian, Louis Armstrong:

When you're smilin', when you're smilin'
The whole world smiles with you

Being in the presence of those who can make a piano sound like a smile brings sunshine too, even on dark days.

KATRINA

The Big One

On the morning of Monday, August 29, 2005, I glanced at the front page of the *Town Talk*, the daily newspaper published in Alexandria, Louisiana. We had been lucky to find a room at a bed and breakfast in Mansura in Central Louisiana to which we had fled the night before. Referring to New Orleans, the headline seemed to justify our hurried escape:

THIS IS THE BIG ONE
Experts Expect Storm to Turn New Orleans into Atlantis

For years there had been predictions from scientists that if a future hurricane would hit the city from an exact direction, roughly heading up the path of the Mississippi River, at a certain intensity, Category 5, the consequences would be deadly for the city as levees broke and flood waters poured onto the land. New Orleans, a town developed below sea level, would, in effect, drown.

Storms had targeted the city before, but there has always been the prayed for last minute turn or weakened wind that lessened the ravage. But one day, we were warned there will be "The Big One."

According to the accompanying *Associated Press* story, "When Katrina hits New Orleans today, it could turn one of America's most charming cities into a vast cesspool tainted with toxic chemicals, human waste, and even coffins released by floodwaters from the city's legendary cemeteries."

And then, as the AP quoted various experts, the news got even worse:

By Tuesday vast swaths of New Orleans would be under water up to thirty feet deep.
In the French Quarter, the water could reach twenty feet, easily submerging the district's iconic cast-iron balconies and bars.
Sixty to eighty percent of the city's houses will be destroyed by wind. Most of the people who live in and around New Orleans could be homeless.

Ivor van Heerden, deputy director of LSU's Hurricane Center added, "We're talking in essence of having a refugee camp of a million people."

That Sunday morning before we left New Orleans, a friend, living alone, called and lamented that she wished someone could tell her what to do. She eventually decided to head to Chicago where she had friends.

By late afternoon that Monday, television coverage fed statewide from New Orleans stations was providing a dash of hope. There were winds and many knocked down tress, but not as bad as expected. The worst singular incident was the century old Southern Yacht Club, which was blistering in a ravaging fire. Overall, though, it looked like we could be returning home by Wednesday.

And then came the news that would change our lives and the hopes for the city: The levees had broken. The city was being overcome by rushing water. No one was going home anytime soon.

A couple of days later, we were watching coverage of the devastation from the B&B's kitchen. Two sisters from the river parishes, each around forty, looked forlornly at the depressing scene. They had a verbal exchange which will always be stamped into my Katrina memories, "Every time I look at those scenes" one said of the coverage, "I want to cry." "Me too," the sibling replied, "but I am afraid if I start, I will never stop."

I could have added my own "me too" to that conversation.

In the end Katrina, because of the broken levees, was plenty bad, though not as devastating as speculated. It was the "Almost Big One" but not *The* Big

One which could be in our future, though we will face it with better flood protection and better built housing.

We were not back in our home until April, and there was lots of fixing that needed to be done. One sign of the neighborhood returning to life was restaurants reopening. No offices for attorneys, doctors, or accountants caused more buzz than an illuminated "OPEN" sign outside a cafe.

Oh, and the friend who called wishing someone could tell her what to do: while in Chicago she met a guy, fell in love, got married, and had a child. I wish I had been the one to have given her that advice.

Pondering the Danziger Verdicts

Someone asked me what I thought about the 2011 verdicts in the Danziger Bridge case. The first word that came to mind was "tragic." Tragic for the convicted and their families; beyond tragic for the victims and their families.

If there was any light at all, it was that the justice system worked. The jury got it right. Clearly there was a cover-up by New Orleans police after two seemingly suspicious but innocent Black men at the Danziger Bridge had been shot and killed, and several people seriously injured during the turmoil of the hurricane; clearly the "civil rights" of the victims were violated. But the jury also ruled that the convicted did not intend to create murder. The jury was right about that too. Danziger was about a whole chain of circumstances gone amuck.

Prisons around the world are filled with people who faced bad circumstances and did the wrong thing. Crimes must be punished, but what nags at me is a variation of what is commonly called, "the Katrina defense." The tension created in the aftermath cannot be overlooked. To me, the most grievous problem was the total absence of leadership. The mayor at the time, we would learn, had lost control. The police chief at the time had melted down. True, the police acted on their own, but there was no specter of someone in charge who they feared having to answer to; no voice in their head saying, "don't do that"; no precedent for restraint. Indeed, in the uncertain days after Katrina some of the officers thought they were being heroic.

I talked to former US Attorney Jim Letten after the convictions. He was emphatic that the verdicts would end the "culture of secrecy" within the department and that officers would know that protecting and serving included coming forth with the truth. Barbara "Bobbi" Bernstein, the Civil Rights specialist out of Washington who handled the case echoed the sentiment, referring to the "thin blue line" under which police routinely protected their own in defiance of the truth.

There were no human winners at Danziger. Family members of the victims who say that the verdicts bring "closure" will find that they will not. The convicted will spend many years wishing they had been among those who simply abandoned the force at the city's darkest hour rather than staying on duty.

Yes, the truth won, but too often in life even victory is disturbing.

Class Action: Katrina Versus Schools

During the first few days after Katrina, we were staying at a bed and breakfast in the Avoyelles Parish town of Mansura. We were lucky to get a room since most of the people were relatives of the owners, including two sisters from the river parishes, each who brought their own family. A doctor from New Orleans was also there. At night she would do volunteer work in the emergency room at the Marksville Hospital.

From the two sisters, both of whom spoke with delightful Cajun accents, came a statement that I will always remember. That Wednesday after the levees broke, we were all watching the destruction of New Orleans on a wide screen TV. "Every time I see that I want to cry," one sister said. "Me too," her sibling said, "but I am afraid if I start, I will never stop."
A couple of days later both were crying, but for a different reason. People may forget that one of the many troubles caused by Katrina is that it came right when school had just started. Everywhere where there were refugees, there were parents figuring out what to do with the kids and their schooling.

Predictions that the city might not be operative for at least six months aggravated the situation. Those who could, tried to enroll their kids wherever they were or make some other arrangement. In the case of one of the sisters, a relative in California had arranged for a high school aged son to go to school there. So one morning the family gathered in the living room as a sister left to take the son to the Golden State not knowing for how long. All of the family wept. For most school kids, the year ahead held some sort of promise, maybe graduation, a prom or football Fridays. Now all of that was gone, and the kids were heading to another world filled with uncertainty.

In some cases it might have been for the best. A friend who was an education specialist was doing supervisory work in the Avoyelles Parish school system. She told us that many of the poor kids from New Orleans who were taken into the Avoyelles schools were seeing a different side of life. "Here you say 'Yes, sir' and 'Yes, ma'am' to the teachers and everyone wears their shirts tucked in with no droopy pants." She said the kids from New Orleans were getting a level of supervision they had never had before. They might be better off.

Another family had two daughters who attended prestigious New Orleans high schools. Now the schools were closed. A Baton Rouge Catholic school took them in. Their parents, like many now dispersed across the region, now had to think about the long term. Should they buy a home, at least to get them through the year?

From one of the daughters came another statement I will never forget: "This is a hard time to be an adult." She was right, of course, and an occasional tear may have provided some relief.

The Quarter's Katrina Halloween

Three police officers were walking together patrolling the streets of the French Quarter on the afternoon of Halloween 2005. That in itself was not unusual, except that the three were all New York State troopers. As though to not look menacing, they wore pullover shirts with the badge insignia on the chests. I stopped and thanked them for being there.

With the city still flattened from the Katrina levee break, the French Quarter was one of the few places where there was activity, though in a different way. Refrigerators, taped shut so as to not allow the grossness within to eke out, lined the old sidewalks. That sickening moldy stench was still pervasive, though there was one bit of good fortune along Decatur Street. Café Du Monde had reopened and the glorious whiffs of beignets and café au lait added badly needed fragrance to the air. Emergency workers who camped out in nearby tents were drawn by the smell.

Coop's Place was one of the few restaurants open, though serving a limited menu, so limited that nothing could be offered that utilized tap water. Greens could not be washed, so there were no salads. Fresh brewed iced tea? How about a Coke?

Locals were gathering at the Napoleon House bar, sitting at one of the outside tables when they could, telling their Katrina stories to anyone who would listen. Business throughout the Quarter was, for the most part, non-existent except for one local artist who was gleeful that FEMA workers took a fancy to his work and had been good customers.

There was no denying the despair and uncertainty that surrounded the neighborhood. The streets were silent in ways that they should not be. There was no calliope song echoing off the old buildings; no rhythm from an approaching brass band, but the people of the Quarter were determined. Only two months after the levees broke, there was going to be an informal parade that night, come hell or, well, whatever.

It must have been around 11:00 p.m. when we returned to the Quarter where we spent the evening in the apartment of a friend who had found safety in the highlands of North Carolina. While we were away, there had been a burst of celebration like an azalea bud suddenly popped open. The streets were littered, but in a good way, with beads and confetti. Witches, ghosts, goblins, and devils sashayed along the streets weaving into bars from which music bounced. Once again there was life in the French Quarter, and it took the night of the dead for it to happen.

National Guardsmen were on patrol the next morning, some having pastries in the same coffee shop where we were. They were from Puerto Rico. I thanked them. Dressed in full fatigues they might have stood out, except nothing in the Quarter ever seems improbable, especially during Halloween 2005.

Before heading back out of town to our Katrina exile, we joined some friends for a picnic at Metairie Cemetery. Even All Saints Day is a celebration in New Orleans, where the rituals of life and death are so entwined.

I have often wondered what the New York State troopers and the Puerto Rican National Guardsmen thought about Halloween in the Quarter. Maybe they learned something about determination. If so, they needed it. In 2017 a devastating Hurricane named Maria would hit Puerto Rico. For the National Guard troops from the island, I hope that they could draw from the New Orleans Halloween experience and find more hope than fright.

A Julia Street Christmas

For most of us the song, "I'll Be Home for Christmas" took on a different meaning just three months after the levees broke. At issue was not so much if we would be home for Christmas but whether we would ever be home at all, or at least back to the place we had once lived.

Our refuge was a small apartment on Julia Street where our usual six-foot-high live tree was replaced by a three-foot artificial tree bought at the Walmart in upstate Alexandria during our exile.

People who we usually visited during the holidays were relocated too, with neither stockings to hang nor chimneys to hang them on.

For many locals the *château du jour* was a trailer provided by FEMA, by then a much-maligned organization that had suddenly become the area's major housing provider.

Conversation came easily at holiday gatherings. Everyone had stories to tell about their recent lives: all stories were compelling, each seeming to top the previous one.

A year earlier, on Christmas Day 2004, snow fell beginning exactly at noon. It was a joyous moment, though a year later some superstitious souls remembered the snow as nature's hex, a disarming moment of brightness as an omen for dark days ahead.

In another country in another century, Charles Dickens's *A Christmas Carol* had created a template for Christmas being a time of goodwill and helping the needy. In 2005, New Orleans was a city of Tiny Tims leaning on their crutches; not only were our lives in shambles, but our community pride was hurt; the Saints were playing in San Antonio; the Hornets (now the Pelicans) in Oklahoma City and (heaven forbid) the Sugar Bowl was held in Atlanta.

But the Yule season by its existence creates its own sauce—a yearning for something benevolent like the British and German soldiers who climbed out of the trenches one Christmas Eve during World War I to sing "Silent Night" together. So in our world, with many roofs topped with blue tarps, the season added a little music, a little sparkle. At midnight of Christmas Eve, we were at St. Patrick's Church for mass. That evening, the priests and the choir staged a show that was unprecedented in its beauty as angelic voices filled the incense-scented chamber with the glory of music that showed the genius and the survivability of mankind.

At that one spot on Camp Street, Christmas morning had arrived gloriously to this mildewed city—and for that hour, at least, all was calm, all was bright.

Saved by Hispanics

During the early days of the Katrina recovery, we called a local construction company for estimates on repairs to our house. Compared to others, the damage was modest, but still four feet of water had scarred the floors; mold was beginning to climb the walls; there were leaky spots in the ceilings throughout and scattered structural needs. After surveying the damage, the company gave an estimate. The cost was exorbitant. As for the floor, they could not do anything until the electricity was back on and that could not happen until the underside of the house was cleared for fear of dead animals and syringes. Did they do that work? "No," was the quick reply.

Then we happened to see a guy who had done some miscellaneous house painting for us before the storm. The native of El Salvador was eager for work. His English was challenged but not his enthusiasm. I showed him the floor. "I can do," he said. "But how about the electricity?" I asked. "I can get a generator," he answered without hesitation. "But under the house?" "We can clear it out."

Then came his rate, which was totally affordable. When could he start? "I will be back later this afternoon."

Working informally as our organizer/contractor, the El Salvadoran and his revolving pick-up crew of mostly Mexicans did an unbelievable job. The floor was restored. The walls were fixed. There were no more spots in the ceiling.

One worker in particular could have qualified as a master carpenter. The work he did in our kitchen bordered on artistic. He did not speak a word of English but if he did, I thought, and if he lived in New Orleans, he could have had a high demand career.

Our house has a second level deck and one day, as I came home, I saw three men doing work there. Each of them had classic Mayan features; including their skin color and size. I smiled when I realized that the deck was being restored by the descendants of the same people who built the Yucatan's Chichén Itzá and the other great Mayan pyramids.

One morning, through the curtain on the front door, I could see the image of a young man standing on the porch carrying what looked like a gun. "Can I help you?" I asked through the door. "I have come to caulk the windows," his Mexican accented voice answered. "Ok," I said, "let me get the key," "That's ok," this total stranger answered, "I have a key." He jangled a ring full. I never hesitated. That's the way it was in Katrina world; life was upside down, strangers with keys were dropping by to caulk. We just had to trust. In the end there was never a reason for me to regret the trust.

Truth is the Mexicans saved us. Our personal recovery would have taken much longer and been much more expensive had it not been for them and that would have altered the speed of the rebuilding of the rest of our lives.

In the months, and even years, after the recovery, it became common to see Hispanic men clustered outside of home improvement stores looking for work. A neighbor complained that the gatherings were unsightly. I argued to the contrary. Blessed are the huddled masses looking for honest work.

Our world was built by virile young men migrating from one country to another hoping for opportunity. Louisiana's Sicilian population descended from men who were imported here to work in the sugar fields once slave labor was lost. They came; sent money home; many intended to return to the old country; many stayed.

My dad was also an example. He was raised poor in rural French-speaking Central Louisiana. There were no jobs. Because of a sister who had come to New Orleans earlier, he moved to town hoping for a chance. I am only here now because he found it.

We know that the burgeoning Mexican population is a delicate issue; particularly in border states. Just as in any place where there is an influx of one mostly poor population on another, there will be serious social problems. It is a timeless story. Nevertheless, it disappoints me to see people degraded as ammunition for political discourse.

I have been close enough to see the humanity.

Sky in the Eye—A Hurricane Called Zeta

Suddenly everything stood still. I had been watching from the second-floor window facing the branches of an ancient oak that stood higher than the two-story houses that surrounded it. This tree has experienced hurricanes before. Now it was experiencing a storm like few others.

Many hurricanes have raged their way close to the city, but seldom has the actual "eye" of the storm crossed the town. That happened in 1947 and then again in 1965 as part of Hurricane Betsy's core clipped the city and now this day, October 28, in the infamous year 2020. As befitting the year, the storm was an oddball that happened as the hurricane season was supposed to be ending. Instead, the season ran out of the standard names and so had to rely on the Greek alphabet. Who knew, other than Greeks and geeks that a word that started with Z would be fifth in the Greek compilation and not at the end as in our everyday English alphabet. But here we were, awaiting the wrath of Zeta only two months after the L for Laura had raked Southwest Louisiana. Where had the other letters and time gone?

If they disturb a holiday, hurricanes are most likely to mess up Labor Day, as Katrina did, or Independence Day, but not Halloween. This time storm preparation included taking down skeletons and assorted ghouls from front yards rather than sheltering barbecue pits.

Of all of the storm's traits, it will be the location of the eye that will capture a spot in the history books. To earn stripes as a hurricane survivor, a person should have experienced being in the center of an eye. Now we are a region of people who can boast that they have been there.

My experience began almost exactly at 6:00 p.m. As though by command, the tree branches stopped swaying and rested at ease. The rain ceased and there seemed to be streaks of light breaking through the gray sky. Then, strangest of all, I could hear kids laughing.

That sent me downstairs and out the front door onto the porch where I was stunned by the sky. It was a celestial color match that I had never seen before, a pale gold blending into a light purple. All day we had been seeing dark gray, now this, a blast of color. Across the street a mom was leading a group of kids, following in line like a group of baby ducks, for a walk. Two of the tykes were carrying tiny umbrellas, waving them while overjoyed that there was no rain. Neighbors began gathering outside as though liberated. One kid shouted, "Everybody is going for a walk now!"

There was something about the gold and purple sky, however, that suggested that the kids' procession would not last long. The sky at that moment was hauntingly beautiful, but it was also disturbingly fragile. Gradually the colors began to fade to be replaced by another palette of gray. Within a half-hour of being encompassed by Zeta's eye, rain had started again. The branches on the tree renewed their swaying.

We were now experiencing what we had been told about life in the eye of a storm: The center can be very peaceful and clear, but we are standing in a swirl and the back end is approaching. The winds will be from the opposite direction and there will be more of the rain we thought had ended.

What is best about the back side is that it is the beginning of the end. Soon the storm will be totally Mississippi-bound.

I am glad we had experienced the eye but am not in a hurry to meet one again. There are twenty-four letters to the Greek alphabet. I was curious which one was last. May none of us ever have to experience a hurricane named Omega.

SERIOUSLY

Sorrow Along the Bayou

I happened to be standing in front of the family of Terrilynn Monette when her car was pulled out of Bayou St. John Saturday, June 8, 2013. Since the popular grade-school teacher disappeared last March, after a night of celebrating teacher of the year recognition, her absence had become a cause. Search parties had combed City Park, her last known path home, and divers had searched nearby Bayou St. John and nearby lagoons.

On this Saturday afternoon, as word spread about a vehicle being located in the Bayou, people had been gathering on the Wisner Avenue side of the waterway near where Harrison Avenue crosses the water. The activity, barricaded by police, was on the opposite side but easy to see as the winch on a tow truck began to turn slowly, pulling the vehicle whose whereabouts had been a mystery.

Among the family and onlookers, there was the sort of emotional overcharge that I have experienced from those standing in the backroom at a wake. Occasional nervous laughs are mixed with sobs as the mind circles for a place to land.

For the family and friends, there had always been hope—not much, but enough to make them keep their T-shirts with Monette's picture nearby. As the winch turned though, hope was being gutted. No one said much at the dramatic instant when the first glimpse of the hood cleared the waterline. After all these months . . . slowly came the rest of the vehicle—the roof, the trunk—green with algae. Still there was stunned silence. Then came the moment when the entire vehicle was dragged onto the shore. Its license plate, with numbers that confirmed the tragic truth, faced the onlookers on the other side of the water. Here was the moment. In unison Monette's beloved began to cry. They huddled into a group hug.

Hope was over.

Yet from nearby there was applause from another group of bystanders. Despite their grief they were cheering the effort of those who raised the car. Sadness and appreciation often ride the same brainwave.

At that point, many of the group drifted into different arms along the shore. Over on the other side of the Bayou, the car once so widely searched for merely stood there. No one opened a door. There was just a quiet protocol. After a while a deputy coroner came. Following some discussion, a tarpaulin, as though to symbolize privacy, was draped over the car as it was again pulled, this time to the back of a flatbed truck. That move seemed totally decent; sparing the family of what would have been a grim sight.

In such situations people inevitably speak of "closure" though that's a concept I have difficulty grasping. Subsequent investigations would rule that she died of drowning, not murder. Still ahead would be a toxicology analysis. No coroner's report, however, closes memories of a person.

At 3:45 p.m. Saturday, June 8, 2013, the truck carrying Monette's vehicle and remains pulled away. There were scar marks along the Bayou where the car was pulled out. I wondered why such marks were never found where the vehicle went in. There are so many questions, but those would be for trained minds to answer. The moment, though, belonged to the heart.

A Mayor, An Inauguration, Two Crises

May 1, 1978, was a fine day, especially for Dutch Morial, who stood at the place of honor on the grandstand erected in front of City Hall. The crowd watched as Morial, dressed in the traditional white suit of mayors-elect on Inauguration Day, raised his right hand and took the oath. It would forever be noted that Morial was the city's first Black mayor, another note in the record book for a city that had long ago elected first mayors who were: not born in France; Italian, Irish, from upstate, or French but born in America. For this day it was the celebration that mattered.

May 2 was a day of getting down to business. The new administration began to pursue its plans, workers took down the viewing stands and, across from City Hall, some environmentalists were constructing various solar power devices which would be displayed the next day to promote the energy future. Though it was on a Wednesday, it would be called *Sun Day.*

On May 3, the sun would be challenged. It was blocked out by a ceiling of dark clouds, By early morning the rain began. It would not stop. Now in only his forty-eighth hour of governing, Moral presided over a city that was under water. Streets were flooded; rowboats were the vehicle of choice. The airport was closed. People were trapped. Not since Hurricane Betsy in 1965 had the city seen so much water damage. This was not Katrina type flooding where the water came in from levee breaks. This was water from above. Governing a city is always tough. On May 3, the reality had gotten even tougher. There was too much concrete and not enough drainage. Even the city's pride, the Superdome covered land that had nowhere to drain. In a city below sea level, the subsurface pipe system was inadequate. What became forever known as the "May Third Flood" sent a message: without a drainage overhaul, urban flooding was going to be a frequent part of the future.

At a time when he could have been absorbing the glory of being a new mayor, Morial's problems began from the start, and there was more thunder in the distance. The New Orleans Police were threatening to strike; what's more there was talk that, without a settlement, they were going to do so during the Carnival season. Without police for crowd control, there could be no parades; without the parades the tourism-based economy would take a hit. Talks intensified as the season grew near but there was no settlement.

Then came the day when the police walked but they had miscalculated the civic resolve of the krewes who they thought would do anything to parade. Instead, the Carnival captains stood firmly behind Morial. It was a fine moment of people doing the right thing; the mostly White krewes backed the first Black mayor in his effort to break a strike, although early in his career he had been a labor lawyer. Morial knew the pain that the police were feeling, but he also knew that giving in to their demands would have been a financial disaster for the city and given the unions too much control. There were no parades in New Orleans during Carnival season that year, but there was still Mardi Gras, the celebration. On that day, the French Quarter was alive with maskers frolicking through the streets. National Guard troops called in to provide protection tried to stand firm as girls danced around them. The soldiers held back smiles as they glanced at the balconies and saw things for which basic training had never prepared them.

During the course of the strike, Edwin Edwards, serving one of his terms as Governor, received a phone call from Morial. Edwards and Morial were both classic Democrat Moderate-Liberals. They got along well, though the governor had the upper hand with his wit. Answering the phone, Edwards teased Morial with a mock complaint that since he became mayor it had been one problem after another; first the flood, now the police strike. By Ash Wednesday 1979, with Mardi Gras over, the police strike lost its leverage and the striking ended. It was a victory for the mayor.

Within ten months, Morial had faced two major crises beginning on his second full day in office. Inauguration day must have seemed so distant. Now he could use a month of Sun Days.

Mother's Day

Someone told me that Alzheimer's is the worst disease because you lose a person twice. I know when the second time was because of a call from the nursing home that came at 3:15 on a Sunday morning.

I will always wonder though about the first time. Was it during my last trip to the nursing home when her eyes seemed to be fixed on nothing in particular? Or was it a month earlier, when she still seemed to recognize me but then phased into a monologue invoking relatives from her distant past? Was it in February when a stroke compounded her maladies? Or was it in October 2005, when she cried as she saw the mush that Katrina had made of her home. She was still physically able then, but the memory was fading. There would have been mercy in that particular memory being the first to go.

A person's life should not be remembered by how it ended but by how it was lived. A cousin who spoke at the services recalled that this particular life spanned the era when women were more often homemakers. They lived as fully as they could, though their opportunities were fewer. The obituary notice mentioned that her life has been affected at each end by floods. As a child growing up in Central Louisiana, she and her family were refugees living in a Red Cross camp, forced there by the Great Flood of 1927. Then, near the end, there was Katrina.

She was a loving, saintly woman with only one known object of contempt in her life—and it was passionate. The scorn she felt for the magnolia tree that grew on the side of her house could drive her to tears. Its roots would break up the sidewalk and prevent the grass from growing. Its leaves fell, seemingly continuously, clogging the drains. Because the tree stood on the public side of the sidewalk, no axe wielder was allowed to chop it down. She might have elicited the services of a professional tree assassin had I not prevailed out of fear of having to pay her bail.

Katrina did what the law did not allow and that was to eradicate the tree. That was, to her, the storm's only benefit. The high water also destroyed a life's worth of family photographs and documents. Surviving, however, was her classic recipe for mushroom rice. The dish would be recreated for a gathering after the funeral. Lost forever, I am afraid, are the secrets for her signature cabbage rolls and her one-of-a-kind snap beans with pickled meat.

Cooking for others was a way of reaching out. The kitchen was her power base. The spatula was her scepter.

Had I known when I was going to lose her the first time, I might have spent more moments gathering memories and recording her speaking in that lyrical Louisiana French patois, but life moved too quickly.

My hope is that in her waning months when her mind took her to other destinations that they were joyful places where she got to revisit the friends and dreams of her youth. Among the few surviving photographs are some that show what a pretty young woman she was as she set out to build a life and a family. Those were happy times: there were no high waters then, and magnolias were safely in bouquets.

The Incident

I called the police recently to report an accident that did not happen.

My saga began innocently enough in the parking lot of the Rouses Market on North Carrollton. The store is quite popular, especially on Sundays, so much so that I had to inch along through the parking lot to find a space. I was barely moving near the front of the store when a woman shopper, who was on her way out, brushed along my left front fender.

She then turned to me and began yelling, "You hit me! You hit me!" I was stunned, "I did not hit you, ma'am," I replied while trying to maintain composure. "You hit me," she insisted, "I can feel a pain in my back!"

I repeated, "I did not hit you!" She insisted I did and then, as though as an afterthought added, "and I am holding a baby." The infant in her arm, who I took to be a grandchild, had a beaming smile on his face that did not indicate pain.

Just then an SUV pulled up alongside the screaming woman. "Did he hit you?" the van driver, a younger woman, asked with an inflection that revealed a predetermined verdict. "Call the police," the van driver, who had been nowhere around when all this started, yelled. "I did not hit anyone," I yelled back. With traffic building up behind me I decided to move my car to the closest available spot, which was about a dozen vehicles down.

By the time I walked back to where the screaming lady had been she was gone. I saw her getting into her automobile showing no pain and then driving away. The SUV was gone too.

With there being no alleged victim of an alleged accident this story might have ended here, but I was reeling. I did not know if what had happened was a set-up or not, but I did know that if anyone was going to be calling the police it would be me. "Where did the accident happen?" the police operator asked. "Well, the accident really didn't happen I answered, but I wanted to report it in case someone called."

Fortunately, the operator was very professional. I explained the incident to her. She responded with the impassionate details of someone who had heard it all before. Because the incident occurred in the supermarket parking lot that was private property and the police would not investigate. The accuser and I, she said, should exchange phone numbers. That person, of course, was long gone.

In the whole realm of public safety, the incident was trivial but in my universe it was Category 5. I thought about telling the store manager and the security guard about what happened, but then I realized I was not going to arouse much interest over a story about an accident that did not happen.

I did spot a departing shopper who I recognized as having once worked for the city attorney's office. I explained what happened, thinking that maybe he was aware of some obscure law that applied to victimless accidents. He merely smiled and said, "I wouldn't worry about it."

And I shouldn't. But I was angry. I was angry at the woman for trying to commit a fraud. I was angry at her again for exploiting a child in the incident. I was double angry at the woman in the SUV for trying to enflame the incident. And I was angry at whatever social ills and circumstances caused the women to behave the way they did.

I hope the child grows up in a better world than his grandparent. My guess is that this was not the first time the older woman claimed to be an accident victim, her reaction was smooth and seemed programmed as though honed with experience. Maybe one day she will learn that each of the innocent people she accuses feel as though they have been run over, and that they too feel a pain—in their soul.

Franklin Augustus/Nancy Parker: The Pilot and the Passenger

When I last talked to Franklin Augustus, the occasion was a party to commemorate the life of a minority pilot who perished while flying.

Augustus was the pilot of the two-person aircraft in which he and news anchor Nancy Parker were killed. I had the fortune, and ultimately the heartbreak, to know both.

My conversation with Augustus was on a July 2, a date that is remembered for the 1937 disappearance of Amelia Earhart somewhere over the Pacific Ocean. She too was at the controls of a two-person aircraft.

It is relevant to the story to say that Augustus was Black because he was proud to be one of his race who had his own airplane and who, as he boasted, was among the world's few Black stunt pilots. He was also proud of Black aviation history, particularly the Tuskegee Airmen, the heralded all-Black flying squad that distinguished itself during World War II. Augustus was a next generation pilot who cherished the stories of the war-time aviators.

On that July night, a Metairie couple with a fondness for aviation staged a party. Earhart's disappearance is so distanced by time that the atmosphere was festive, including a group sing-along to Kinky Freeman's folk piece about Earhart's flight:

There's a beautiful, beautiful field

Far away in a land that is fair
Happy landings to you, Amelia Earhart

I now wonder if Augustus felt some sort of kinship with Earhart who, like him, was among the few of his particular minority to sit behind the controls. He obviously felt a link to the Tuskegee pilots. That night he talked to me about wanting to glorify the memory of the group. He was hoping for a documentary, a book, at least a magazine article. Our discussion ended an agreement to meet soon. That was the last time I talked to him.

My last conversation with Nancy Parker was also about books. At the time she was working on a children's publication and was looking for how-to information. All the superlatives spoken about her are true. Both Parker and Augustus were interested in kids' causes, including dissuading youth violence. They were both special people.

Fox 8 News faced an impossibly difficult task and handled it with dignity. Situation: What to do when reporting about a horrible accident and you know that a victim is one of your own, but nothing has been verified? Protocol demands some sort of official confirmation before revealing the names of victims. Shortly after the accident at 3:00 p.m. the WVUE newsroom knew that Parker was a passenger and that there were no survivors. Yet the early reporting could only talk about the accident without the details. In a live report from the crash site veteran reporter Rob Masson showed true professionalism as he calmly reported about the incident but could not make any revelations. He did his job well, though anyone who knew what had happened could tell that he was aching inside.

A mutual friend told me how excited Augustus had been because Parker was interested in his story and was going to go flying with him. If only the story could have continued.

The Boot

If your car has not gotten booted lately, you should know the good news is that the process of dealing with it has gotten a lot easier; the bad news is that it is now a lot easier to get booted.

This is a topic I have become more an expert about than I cared to. The latest incident was on the evening of Labor Day, a holiday in the eyes of every government agency in America, except for the booting people who know when folks will be vulnerable. The location was the French Quarter, a happy hunting ground for those in search of cars parked in bootable public spaces. (I can imagine the parking bureau's director of citizen harassment has such holidays circled on the calendar and holds morning pep rallies for the corps of booters.)

Time was that a car was booted only when there was a long list of unpaid violations. Now, in the age of the traffic camera, offenses mass at a speed greater than the violated speed limits. (The start of the school year must be a high holy day for the traffic camera people knowing full well that many people have not yet adjusted to the new hours and rules.) For those who had other ways in mind to spend their three-figure fine, such as paying for school tuition, the numbers mount quickly. We have become a city of scofflaws playing into the hands of the evil booters.

A sheet attached to the driver's side window gave a phone number where an operator, who was amazingly pleasant, being that virtually everyone she talks to is angry, took my card number and then gave me a code which was to be punched on the keyboard located on the side of the boot. Since the boot is on the tire and the tire is on the ground, that required my getting on hands and knees while hoping not to be mugged or swiped by a passing vehicle, all in the name of justice. The code unlocked the boot, but the contraption remained stuck on the tire. It took a passerby who obliviously had plenty experience with boots to help wrestle it off. According to the conditions of getting the code, I had to agree to keep the boot in my trunk, not in the back seat and return it to the booting station within twenty-four hours.

That station is located beneath the Claiborne Overpass at Bienville Street. A sign outside a locked gate instructs you to blow your horn for the attendant. Meanwhile my waiting car was, in the name of justice, a target for speeding turning vehicles. The attendant eventually sauntered to the gate. She seemed totally paranoid. The gate was unlocked only partially, just wide enough for the boot to be slipped to her. There was no conversation, just grunts when needed.

When I had awakened Labor Day morning, I thought the greatest threat to my peace that day would be a tropical storm; it turned out to be the city government.

Nearby a painter's truck had suffered a similar experience; so much for the profit from putting in a day's work—on Labor Day.

I continue to love New Orleans. I just wish its policy makers would not make it so hard to do so.

TRAVEL

The Woman on The Plane

As soon as the main cabin door was closed, I made my move. Though I had already secured an aisle seat, I noticed that the middle section front row behind the bulkhead of this jumbo jet was empty. By moving quickly, not only would I still have an aisle seat, but also more leg room, plus an empty middle seat to allow extra elbow room while crossing the Atlantic.

A nod from a flight attendant assured that my maneuver, though done at a time when we were supposed to be docilely buckled in, was okay. On matters of airplane seats, I am at my most evil, being not only calculating but also selfish. My new location was three seats across, and I really hoped that no one would take either of the other two. That was not to happen though. Before the plane started to move a woman, big of stature, who looked a little disheveled as though she had just run through the airport, claimed the opposite aisle seat.

Quickly, she shoved her carry-on bag into the overhead bin and stashed her purse beneath the seat. Thankfully, the middle seat remained unoccupied.

As the plane rumbled along the tarmac, I conceded to myself that I would have to share middle seat space with the woman and that use of the seat's pull-up tray, which I had hoped to control might have to be time-shared. To my delight, the woman never even glanced at the middle seat. Once we were at cruise level, she read magazines for a while and then fell asleep.

It would be easier for me to do cartwheels down the aisle than to fall asleep in a plane, so I just sat there pleased that I could stretch my legs, flex my arms, use the middle seat tray, and stand up anytime I wanted without getting in anyone's way. Meanwhile the woman slept. She slept through dinner, breakfast, announcements from the pilot, and the shuffle of people standing in line for the nearby restroom. She was even unfazed by two kids three rows back, one who continually screamed and the other who talked at decibel levels higher than the jet engines.

Her sleeping seemed normal, until much later in the flight at that blessed hour when the plane began its descent. The cabin lights were suddenly turned on in the darkened cabin so that the attendants could make sure that everyone was buckled in, their trays were up, and gear was stored. An attendant tried to get the lady to put her purse into the bin, but she wouldn't budge. Gently the attendant shook the woman, but nothing happened. The attendant raised her voice, nudged the woman a little harder, but still nothing. As the plane descended, the attendant gave up, placed the purse in the bin herself and glanced in my direction asking me to tell the woman where her purse was. I nodded.

Suddenly I was the woman's caretaker—and then I had a horrible thought: what if she was, you know, sort of like, well—dead? I stared at her for signs of life. She certainly slept silently. I thought I could detect slight movement but that might have been from the plane. Then I had another thought that I was ashamed of myself for thinking. If she was dead, did that mean that we would not be able to get off the plane until some authorities came in to investigate? Was I now a witness? Would she have survived had she had more access to the middle seat?

I watched her closely as the plane's wheels touched the runway: There was a slight bounce, not harsh, but enough to wake up anyone who might be sleeping, except for the woman who remained in her condition. She stayed that way as the flight attendant welcomed everyone to Charles De Gaulle Airport and gave the present time. This is the moment when most passengers are primed, ready to bolt the plane at first notice, but the woman did not move. If there was going to be questioning, I was hoping the gendarmes could speak English.

After eight hours afloat, the plane approached the arrival gate and came to a stop. Then there was that beloved sound of liberation, the "ping" freeing passengers from captivity. I took another desperate look at the woman and discovered that her subconsciousness was apparently programmed to the ping. Her eyes shot open. She glanced in my direction. "Your purse is in the bin," I told her. After all the time we had spent together I thought I might owe her another comment, but then, "I thought you were dead" seemed a little harsh.

People who are able to sleep so soundly for so long on a plane either have inner peace or lots of pills. I had neither. If only she could have shared whatever she had with the kids in the third row.

Stories from Seat Level

Like the flashing scenery outside, you sit long enough in any form of long-distance transportation and many life moments pass by:

After graduating from high school, a buddy of mine and I took a trip to Los Angeles in the back of a Greyhound bus. I will always remember the cowboy who got on in Phoenix. He sat behind us, and for the rest of the trip he excitedly told anyone who would listen that he and his wife were reuniting. She was going to meet him in Los Angeles and they were going to try again. Over and over we heard the story with the excitement building as the bus neared the terminal.

I last saw the man as we were leaving the station. He was sitting on a waiting area chair, his head was hanging down showing the pained look of someone who had been bucked into a freefall. There had been no one to meet him. This cowboy would still be riding alone.

Then there was, many years ago, the train trip from New Orleans to Chicago on the City of New Orleans. We were riding coach where an elderly Black woman with gaunt skin and her gray hair in a bun sat behind us. She was going to Effingham in Southern Illinois, but since her kids could not pick her up until two days later, and since she had plenty spare time, she would take the ride down to New Orleans. The lady had never been there before so her plan, as she repeated many times during the eight-hundred-mile ride, was to take advantage of the six-hour layover, go to a nearby restaurant and have "a nice salad and an iced tea."

Good morning America, how are you? From Memphis, Jackson, and into Louisiana the salad and tea were heralded. Unfortunately, south of Jackson a freight train had broken down. The City of New Orleans was diverted to sidetracks, an act that substantially delayed movement so that it finally arrived in New Orleans just as the northbound train was leaving.

I last saw the lady being hurried by a conductor to the departing train having had neither food nor drink nor time to see New Orleans. I hoped that the salads were nice and the tea sweet in Effingham.

Then there was a recent flight from Washington, DC. Two couples sat in the back. One of the women was especially loud, so I could not help but hear that they were from one of Louisiana's river parishes. The lady explained to a passenger that they were returning from a tour of New England. "It was so beautiful," she said, "We went through Maine, Massachusetts, Vermont, Rhode Island, and Cincinnati."

"Cincinnati!!" I thought to myself as other passengers within earshot turned their heads and stared at her.

Then the woman caught herself. "I mean Cincinnaticus." There were still confused stares. She paused again: "I mean Connecticut."

Give the woman credit though; at least she knew to take the plane to Louisiana rather than to Louisville.

The Praying Man

This was the flight that was supposed to be relaxing. We were on the last leg of our trip as the Jet Blue plane took off from New York's JFK Airport heading through the night to New Orleans. Through crafty booking I had secured the first two seats on the left side. My strategy was to relax and watch the History Channel on one of the TV monitors provided for every seat while occasionally glancing out the window.

All was calm as the jet climbed to cruising altitude. Before issuing the ping signaling that it was ok to move about the cabin, the pilot announced that the flight would be smooth and that we should arrive on time. "Ping."

Then something disconcerting happened. A bearded man wearing Muslim clothes approached the area in front of me, faced the door, and began praying. His praying was dramatic as he continually bowed toward the door,

All stereotypes aside, this is not what a person wants to see when sitting in an airplane. I realized that on a southbound jet the left door faces east in the general direction of Mecca to where his prayers were directed.

I will admit to certain uneasiness as I watched him pray, a feeling that was intensified as he dropped to his knees and the paces of his chants increased. I glanced back at the flight attendants who were working the beverage carts at the back of the plane and apparently oblivious to what was going on. I looked across that aisle where college students who showed no reaction occupied the first two rows. They were, I reasoned, overly programmed with political correctness. But on the third row there was a man whose eyes were as wide as mine as he gazed toward the door. I had already decided that if the praying man made one unusual move, I would leap to restrain him. I could tell that I had a colleague in the third row.

But then the prayers stopped, and the man quietly walked back to his seat. By this time a flight attendant had worked her way up front. I anxiously gestured at her toward the door. She understood my telepathy and said, "Oh, I know, he asked me if it would be ok to do that. I said it was alright."

At that point I might have returned to the History Channel and even gotten a glass of wine, but then the praying man approached the front of the plane again. This time he went into the restroom—the one right behind the pilots' door. I could only stare at the door, waiting for him to come out. I wondered if there was anything beneath his tunic that got past security.

He was in the restroom for what seemed like a long time. If he had gone in over Pennsylvania surely we must be approaching West Virginia, but then he came out and walked back to his seat just as quietly as he had before.

This was not the relaxing flight I had hoped for, and I was also beginning to feel a little guilty. Was I wrong for feeling so anxious? At least the guy in the third row could feel my pain.

Finally, the flight might have settled down but then there was another development. A flight attendant rolled the beverage cart in such a way that it blocked access to the front of the plane. That done, a pilot came out, looked around, and went to the restroom while an attendant went into the flight deck. After the first pilot went back to his seat, the other pilot came out and got a cup of coffee. He also gave what I perceived to be a smiling glance directed at me. Surely the attendant had told him about the nervous passenger. I was comforted at least that all the crewmembers seemed at ease.

As the plane began its descent, I had a lot to think about. Had I been guilty of stereotyping? Yes. Was it a stereotype that would come naturally to most people? Yes. Had I acted insensitively? No. Would it have been a sensitive gesture on the part of the praying man to be aware of the anxiety that his actions might cause? Perhaps.

Instead of watching the History Channel that evening, I had experienced some of history's fallout. We were walking toward the airport garage when I last saw the praying man. He was walking toward the exit carrying no luggage but only a small handbag.

His world seemed very lonely. With the passing of time maybe ease between cultures will truly have a prayer.

Southwest Roulette

My strategy for this flight on Southwest Airlines from New Orleans to Baltimore was to head to the back of the plane. Because I am one of those finicky people who are obsessed with never having a middle seat, I inquired and learned from the gate agent that the flight was 70 percent full. That being the case, I reasoned that if I went to the back, most of the passengers would be siphoned off as they passed through the front part of the plane leaving me with arm room from 30 percent emptiness.

As I neared the back, I put my overcoat and overnight case in an overhead bin, and then, just to fully implement my plan, I sat a few seats further back. I buckled myself into the aisle seat hoping that the other two seats would remain vacant. My plan would backfire even worse than I imagined.

There must have been a rush of new passengers after I checked with the gate agent because the plane was practically full, including two hunky guys who sat in the seats next to me. From New Orleans across the South, I flew feeling an elbow at my ribs.

My favorite sound in the world is that "ping" from the cockpit indicating that it is okay to get off the plane. I bulldozed myself up to the baggage bin, grabbed my overcoat and suitcase, and plodded toward the entrance.

Our destination was Washington but because the trip was last minute, it was more economical to arrive through Baltimore. Or at least it would have been had the freeway linking the two cities not been jammed with traffic and slowed by accidents. Our taxi driver at least had a heartwarming story. He was a native of one of those "-stan" countries that made up the former Soviet Union. The only way he was able to move to America was through the intercession of Bill Clinton when he was president. My heart would have been warmed even more had the fare only been fifty dollars instead of the one hundred dollars caused by the slow movement. The taxi driver was certainly learning to appreciate capitalism.

After settling in the hotel room, I had to run an errand, so I grabbed my overcoat and headed toward the elevator. While going down I noticed something strange. Somehow during the flight, either the coat had shrunk, or I had gotten bigger. I knew it wasn't the latter given Southwest's peanut-based food service. I reached into the coat's pocket and pulled out a set of keys that was not mine.

Back in the room, I came to terms with what happened. Another passenger with a coat that looked exactly like mine had put his luggage in the same bin. We had walked away with each other's coat. Worse yet, not only did I have his boarding pass for a flight to Connecticut but also his keys which included those for his car and his house.

Dreading the voicemail hell that comes with calling a 1-800 number, I tracked down Southwest's lost and found department where I actually linked up with a real person who said she could not give me the passenger's phone number but agreed to place a call and to leave a message. I gave her my phone number along with instructions to have him leave an address and I would mail his coat to him and then he could mail mine to me.

Later that night I checked my home number. The man had called and said that although he had no keys when he arrived in Connecticut, he called a son who picked him up and had a spare key to his house. He left his address. The only problem was that he no longer had my coat. He left that with Southwest's lost and found in Baltimore.

Once again, I weathered voicemail and got another real and live person. Southwest had my coat, and they would mail it, all I had to do was give a FedEx credit number. The hotel helped me ship the other coat to Connecticut, but for that I had to give another shipping credit number, but at least the issue was resolved.

At first, I felt guilty for taking the wrong coat, but then I realized the other guy probably got off before me so he made the initial wrong grab. It was his fault! In retrospect, I wish I had sent his coat to him COD but no, I absorbed the cost. The bill, I would later learn, for the combined shipping was ninety dollars.

There was also the emotional cost of almost three hours' worth of angst which I estimate to be in the six figures.

Curiously, none of this would have happened had I just taken a seat in the front of the plane. I would have been crowded, but I was crowded anyway, plus it took me longer to get out. All was not lost though. I did at least beat the system in one way. Somewhere over Virginia, when the flight attendant passed by—I got an extra bag of peanuts.

Two Women in Burqas

Two women dressed, head to toe, in black burqas were getting on the same Delta flight, from Paris to Atlanta, that I was boarding.

Yes, I know about the proper political correctness and the unfairness of stereotypes, but there are some things that make fellow flyers squeamish:

France is a country that does not allow faces to be fully covered in a public place, so you might think that the rules would be more stringent on a plane, but apparently not. The women and their entourage were stopped at a pre-entry security area but after a few moments of checking documents, they were allowed to board. Travelling with them were two men plus two toddlers (a boy and a girl) and a baby. Only the women were dressed culturally. The rest of the family was in totally western casual garb that made the juxtaposition to the two women even stranger.

Whoever booked their tickets obviously knew planes. They had secured a row of seats behind a bulkhead—the wall that divides sections. That's a good place for someone travelling with a newborn because the wall has two hooks that can be used to attach a crib. The disadvantage to the location is that it is next to the restrooms, so people tend to congregate at that spot. As I did the same, I tried to be discreet in assessing the group. Both of the men looked like they could be comfortable at a football game tailgate party; the two toddlers were occupied with coloring books. The baby was totally cute, with puffy cheeks, and slept peacefully. Then there were the two women in black. They merely sat in their seats, for nine hours, their world view limited through the mesh that covered their eyes.

More than uneasiness, I felt sorry for them. What must it be like to live in a world in which even their children have more freedom than they have?

Then I noticed that one of the burqa women did something very modern. She pulled out an iPhone and began scrolling with her thumb. As the apps flashed by, she showed lots of scrolling experience and many apps to choose from. Though she could use none of them while in airplane mode, the rolling apps at least provided distraction through the black mesh.

Down the row, the toddlers continued with their crayons. I wondered if they ever asked why Mom was dressed that way.

Because they were totally covered, there was little to be learned about the two women except for a fleeting moment. One of the women, the one with the iPhone, briefly turned her head toward me. For an instant our eyes made contact. She had strong dark eyes that seemed to be outlined with light makeup. I would guess she was in her early thirties. The eyes seemed sad, but that might have just been the context in which I was seeing her. From what I could tell, she looked like she was quite pretty. Then she turned away.

As the plane began its descent the baby was still soundly asleep. Maybe one day he will wake up to a more just world.

Nashville Night

A Saturday night, several years ago, and I was alone on lower Broadway Street in Nashville. The street jumps with the sound of bands performing inside the many honky-tonks that line the way. Their music is country, a sound that plays to the heart and that totally relates to being alone on a Saturday night—especially in Nashville.

Some honky-tonks are too crowded to enter, but that night I squeezed myself into Robert's Western World past the band at the entrance, then weaved near the tables and alongside the bar. My strategy was to hope that a bar stool would open, claim it, order a cheeseburger and a longneck (always a longneck on Broadway) and then hope that the service would be slow so that I could have more time to hear the band.

Honky-tonk bands play for tips, but a band passing the hat on Broadway in Nashville is better than headline groups elsewhere. For dreamers, Broadway in Nashville is like the other Broadway, if you can make it there you can make it anywhere.

My strategy was working: a bar stool cleared, and I had ordered a cheeseburger and a Bud longneck, now if only the counter lady, who was working several orders across the crowded bar, could take her time.

Robert's is owned by a Brazilian country singer named JesseLee Jones. He and his band perform there many evenings. Jones specializes in the songs of the late Marty Robbins who had a sound that few people could duplicate. I requested my all-time favorite country and western song, "Don't Worry 'Bout Me" and Jones sang it perfectly. It was as though I had closed my eyes and Marty Robbins walked in from the Grand Ole Opry to sing the song.

Across the street was, for many years, the Ernest Tubb Record Shop, where on my first visit the guy behind the counter had been from Shreveport. The upstate town was once the home of the *Louisiana Hayride,* a Saturday night radio broadcast, like the *Grand Ole Opry,* where the careers of Elvis and Hank Williams were boosted before they became stars in Nashville.

Down the street and around the corner is Printer's Alley, a strip known for its more avant-garde nightclubs, including a place called the Bourbon Street Blues & Boogie Bar. It was there that a waitress named Gretchen Wilson was urged to sing a few songs. She was so good that she was encouraged to get a recording contract by two of the bar's customers, songwriter/singers Big Kenny and John Rich. The three would become part of the MuzikMafia. In 2004 the Mafia had three super hits, Wilson's "Redneck Woman" and "Here for the Party" and an unbelievable country/rap number by Big and Rich called "Save a Horse (Ride a Cowboy)." Incredibly, the words Bourbon Street and mafia remain linked, sometimes even in a positive way.

My favorite spot, though, is Robert's.

I nursed my longneck while waiting for the cheeseburger that, as I had hoped, had been backlogged by the other orders. Robert's interior decorating motif consists of western boots with pairs on display from the walls. For the price of a burger and a beer, plus a few dollars in the tip jar, I had an hour's worth of entertainment. Now, like in a good country music song, it was time for the heartbreak. I had to leave.

Outside, Broadway had become even busier and the beat spilling from the nightclubs had grown. The night was in full motion, a perfect setting for being lonely again.

Taken for a Ride in a Stretch Limo

Isn't there a point when stretch limousines become buses disguised as limousines?

Recently I noticed one of those vehicles going down Canal Street. Riding in a limousine once meant something special, but that was when a limo was a stately sedan. Nowadays, for every person that can be packed into a vehicle, the less special it gets.

At the very back there is a seat, which can accommodate maybe three people snugly. At the front is the driver who is in another time zone. To the left, an uncomfortable long padded bench runs along the side. Passengers sitting on it are subject to be jostled by centrifugal force when the vehicle makes turns. To the right is the limo's wow factor, a liquor bar, usually outlined with fiber optic lights, designed, I presume, to give a disco look. Using the bar is a challenge since the vehicle is moving. A bartender would have to sit on the floor with knees in his back to effectively concoct a drink more sophisticated than opening a beer.

As I watched the limo negotiate the turn at North Carrollton Avenue, I thought about my recent unanticipated experience inside one of those centipedes on wheels:

Our flight home from Reno wasn't until mid-afternoon. We wanted to see Lake Tahoe but because of schedules and availability, the only option was to hire a car. It was an extravagance, but way cheaper than flying back from New Orleans to see the lake. Tahoe was about an hour away. As planned, we could spend a couple of hours there and then be driven to the airport.

We thought we were getting a Town Car—what showed up was a black stretch limousine. Since there were only two of us, we certainly could not complain about legroom. The bar had flasks of hooch, but I wasn't in the mood. There were leftover Cokes from a previous party. I poured one, not because I necessarily wanted it, but because since I had paid for it, I felt compelled to. (Not unlike feeling obligated to go for a second helping at a buffet.)

There must have been thirty feet between us and the driver who was a young woman dressed in a chauffeur uniform. She tried to be informative, but she spoke softly, and her sound waves did not always make it to the back.

There were some spots along the lake that we could not visit because the curves to get there were too narrow for the vehicle's length. Fortunately, there was one overlook that was approachable. As we pulled in, we were certainly conspicuous. Among the SUVs, campers, Jeeps, and bikes, our limo looked like it had gotten lost returning from a prom.

Road construction near Tahoe City would slow our progress, so much so that from the front came the barely audible sounds of our driver saying we would have to cut the tour short to get to the airport in time. So, our craft turned away from the lake and headed over hills, into valleys, through plains, and alongside Carson City to the Reno airport.

I am one of those finicky flyers who hates seeing a stretch limousine or a bus pull up to the departure area at an airport for fear that it is carrying a load of people who will be crowding the flight I am in. Any concern our arrival may have caused for fellow finicky flyers was relieved when the just the two of us climbed out.

At the airport, we learned that our flight had been delayed by an hour. So, we just sat and waited.

Too bad we didn't have a car to show us around.

~~~~~~~~~~~~~~~~~~~~~~~~~~~~~~~~~~~~

Lost in Jackson Hole

~~~~~~~~~~~~~~~~~~~~~~~~~~~~~~~~~~~~

We had two hours on our own in Jackson, Wyoming, the town which is known for the surrounding valley formed by the majestic Teton Mountains. In Old West parlance, a valley was known as a "hole," so the area would be referred to as Jackson Hole.

Our Tauck tour bus was parked in a public lot not far from various shops and bars. One of the latter was called the Million Dollar Cowboy where the bar stools were topped with saddles. We had to settle for a table. Our drink choices included a "Cowboy Mule" or a "Cowgirl Cosmo," both made with huckleberry vodka. Had there been more time, we might have split a "Million Dollar Bison Burger," perhaps with an order of "Bovine and Swine Beef Sticks," but the clock was ticking.

A friend had recommended that we stop by the Wort Hotel, an Old West establishment where the cattle barons must have made deals in the lobby. We were able to find the hotel after a few wrong turns; then we looked for a gift shop before deciding to spend the remaining time on a bench in a nearby park.

When it was getting close to the return time, we thought we knew a shortcut, so we went in that direction.

You might think that in a town with a population of only eleven thousand that there should be no chance of losing our way, but the population size doesn't matter as much as the street names. In Manhattan (which has 148 times the population as Jackson Hole) the streets are numbered in sequence. So, if you're on 34th Street and you're looking for 37th, you know how to find your way. Also, there are landmarks including towering buildings. In Jackson there is no notable sequence to the street names and the only towers are the Tetons in the distance.

Concerned, we stopped at a corner, looked around, and faced the realization: We were lost. We're usually better at preventing this type of situation, but the circumstances were not in our favor. Earlier that day we had taken a raft trip down the Snake River (full disclosure: a wimpy raft ride; not white water) during which we saw several eagles and, most of all, a moose. We snapped pictures with my iPhone obsessively, so that by the afternoon, the battery was drained. We found out later that Halsey, our tour guide, worriedly tried to call us. She could have solved everything, but of course our phone was dead. If only we hadn't seen the moose.

I had hoped to see a friendly police officer pass by, but the force must have been out chasing cattle rustlers. There were none to be spotted. Peggy noticed a gallery across the street and went to ask for directions. I stood at the corner hoping for help.

Then, something strange happened. A convertible sports car came racing up the street; turned the corner and stopped near me. The driver hopped out of the car. He was a hunk, a really handsome guy dressed in a suit. Then he asked me a question that was unbelievable. "Are you on the Tauck tour and lost trying to get back to the bus?" I was stunned. There was nothing on me that said "Tauck." I guess we looked a little like tourists, but not so much, plus there were plenty other tourists in town.

He told me to go down the side street for one block then three blocks to the right. He then hurried back to his convertible and sped away. It happened so fast I did not have a chance to ask him questions such as, "Who are you?" "How did you know?" And "Why are you wearing a coat and tie?" (I reckon he was the only person in Wyoming wearing a suit that August afternoon.)

Having gotten no insights from the gallery, we set out following the convertible driver's instructions: one block straight ahead; three blocks to the right. As we reached the third block, we could see a figure in the distance standing on the corner, waving her arms. It was Halsey.

We were like sailors adrift on a raft suddenly spotting a seagull in the distance and knowing that land was nearby.

It must have been around 4:25 p.m. when we got in the bus. I apologized to the fellow passengers for being late. They were good natured about it, perhaps reasoning, incorrectly, that I had too many "Cowboy Mules."

All was well, except I could not forget about the man in the car. How did he arrive at the corner where we were at that very moment? And instead of my telling him our situation, he told me.

One thought was that maybe Halsey knew him and had called for help. Over breakfast the next morning I confronted her, eyeballs to eyeballs and asked her if she knew who he was. "I have no idea," she responded. Neither did the bus driver.

When I told the story to our fellow travelers, someone would usually suggest, jokingly, that maybe he was a guardian angel.

That of course, is nonsense. We are talking about mythical spirits versus rational analysis and reasoning. Besides, angels do not drive sporty convertibles.

Or do they?

Lady Liberty Up Close

We were up early to see a lady who would be standing on a small island in the harbor. According to the cruise ship's captain we should be passing the Statue of Liberty around 7:00 a.m. The cruise director suggested instead 6:45 a.m., just to be sure. We were on the seventh-floor deck by 6:30 a.m. We were not alone. About fifty other passengers also thought that this would be a special moment. Some had draped one of the ship's white robes for an extra layer of warmth. All stood at the rails with their cameras in focus.

New York Harbor, even in the wee hours of a quiet Sunday morning, is dazzling with images, some real; others of the mind. The latter including early steamships chugging in after days crossing the Atlantic. What must the immigrants have thought as they too waited see the statue? Or how about the boatloads of soldiers returning from the great wars, some carried on stretchers; all relieved that they had survived. A tugboat passed nearby, its front deck evoking images of *Funny Girl* Barbra Streisand pleading in song for life not to rain on her parade.

To the left (ok, the portside) was New Jersey, its notables including Frank Sinatra, Jersey Boys, the Sopranos and the spot where Aaron Burr shot Alexander Hamilton in a duel. To the starboard is the jagged skyline of New York City in which stand Broadway, Yankee Stadium, Central Park and, at Trinity Church, the spot where Alexander Hamilton is buried.

(Robert Fulton the inventor of the steamboat, is buried in the plot next to Hamilton's but gets little attention these days since Hamilton, the Legacy, became a Broadway star.)

"There she is!" one of the passengers shouted. Yes, there it was as the ship negotiated a bend. With her outstretched right arm carrying a golden flame atop a torch, "Lady Liberty," as her closest friends call her, was already busy greeting arrivals.

I fully expected to marvel at this monument, and I did, until I happened to glance toward the starboard at the continuing pageantry of the Manhattan skyline. Standing out was a sleek and stylish building climbing to 104 stories making it the tallest building in the hemisphere. No building, perhaps none on the world, triggers as much emotion as does the glowing new One World Trade Center boldly making a statement by its presence.

Our ship docked at a spot not far from where the *Titanic,* had it ever arrived, would have berthed. The harbor was getting busy with the traffic from boats of all sorts, each greeted by the lady.

Another day at the nation's front door was underway.

To have been standing at a spot in the harbor flanked by the statue and the World Trade Center, both in their own ways symbols of hope and renewal, was a sensory overload, each demanding visual attention. But the center won out. In its own way, it too carries a torch.

Getting Back from Broadway

Theaters throughout New York's Broadway district were letting out for the evening but the rain was not relenting—neither was the winter cold which came in blasts. Suddenly we were among hundreds competing for a dry way to get to where we were staying. There were taxis, many of them, but every one was filled and heading away. We could have taken the subway, but the underground station was several blocks away and I wasn't sure what to do when I got there. We could have prearranged to hire a car. (Next time I will try to remember to do that, and to bring Bill Gates with me to split the tab. And I was not yet Uber literate.) We were cold, wet, and helpless on Broadway.

Then, of all the monologues spoken on Broadway that night, none was as beautiful as the one delivered in an Eastern Europe accent by a young man standing on the corner: "Would you like a ride?" he asked.

Looking through the forest of transportation options I had failed to see the critters, the pedicabs, working their way through the crowds. Our destination was about twenty blocks away, yet the driver agreed to take us. His vehicle is essentially a big tricycle. We plumped into the two seats in the back. Then he zipped a plastic sheet that surrounded us. For a moment I felt claustrophobic as we were sealed into cellophane like a pair of potato chips. Our driver began pedaling. It would have been better had I not been looking. He began by actually turning head-on into the traffic and then weaving his away across the street to the left lane. Then he straightened his path. His legs, pumping like pistons, propelled us up 8th Street. He was not, as might have been expected, a hunk with bulging muscles, instead he was an average-sized kid with lots of gumption trying to make a buck. (Four per minute; but it was worth it.).

Unlike us, he had no protection from the rain. He pedaled into the elements, hauling us though a soggy night. From a taxi's perspective, the streets of Manhattan seem to be level. As seen from a pedicab the truth is revealed: the Island was carved from hills. In the direction we were heading, there was a gradual elevation. Our driver was standing on the pedals working up the force, chugging with each down stroke.

By the time we got to our destination, the rain had subsided. From there, we only had to walk across the street then continue about a half block. He unzipped us. Once I added in his well-deserved tip the cost was more than had we actually hired a car, nevertheless, without him we might still be standing on Broadway waiting for the taxis to return.

There was a median in the street where we waited to cross next to a traffic light. We talked about how lucky we were to be arriving dry. Meanwhile the traffic light was about to turn red. Onrushing taxi drivers sped up whizzing near the curb where puddles had accumulated. There must have been four taxis in a row, each shooting a splash into the air roughly equivalent to surfing waves. The water formed a canopy over us and then crashed, leaving us thoroughly soaked,

In the end we were drenched, but at least in the spirit of Broadway, there had been drama.

Dangling Over Mount Etna

For twenty-three years I had avoided the experience. Now I had no choice. There was smoke rising from the volcano and the only way to get off the mountain was to take the ride.

This saga began in May 1984 when the World's Fair opened in New Orleans. I loved attending the fair though not necessarily taking its rides. One trip on the monorail had been good enough for me, especially since the doors got temporarily stuck closed the time I did ride; as for the "gondola," zero times was the number I strived for.

Throughout the months of the fair, nothing haunted me like the gondola—a cable-driven system of round capsules that moved across the river from two hundred feet above the water. My phobias were many. I might have overcome the fear that a falling capsule would plunge into the river like a bomb were it not for the memory of the fair's opening days when the mechanical wheel that moved the cable broke and passengers were left suspended in their glass shell. Just past the point when the gondola began its descent over the midway, I could actually see a man in a capsule stuck inside like some medieval criminal being displayed before the town's people. "I think I will wait until the lines get shorter," I kept telling myself throughout the season. The fair's closing day provided some relief. "I wanted to go, but the lines were too long" would be the official explanation—but then it was announced that the system would remain open as a high-wire form of rapid transit. I knew I would have to take the ride someday, just as someday I would have to face a prostate exam or have a root canal treatment. Mercifully, the demand among locals to fly between Algiers and downtown was insufficient so that the system quickly closed for good. No more would I be taunted by the sight of glass beads bobbing in the skyline, at least until May, 2007, as our tour bus ascended Mount Etna in Sicily.

From a parking area located about half-way up the volcano we were going to have to take a cableway up to a base camp, from which four-wheel drive buses would haul us nearer to the top. While others gazed at the smoke billowing from Etna, I was fixated on the cableway which looked just like the World's Fair gondola of yore. Was there any way out of this?

Surprisingly the wind was an ally. Because of gusts the cable system was closed for the moment so we would have to take a four-wheel drive to the top. Saved by the breeze.

Riding up a volcano in a bus rumbling over untamed roads made me nostalgic for the potholed streets of New Orleans.

Volcano tops are nice places to visit. They are eerily awesome, like a lunar landscape. They are also great places to leave. The temperature was below freezing, and windblasts of near ninety miles per hour peppered us with lava dust. We were among the first in the bus for the return trip to the base camp where I looked for the four-wheel that would carry us to the bottom. Then came the news: No bus, the cable was now running. There was no other way down.

If the capsule had fallen, we would have bounced a bit over lava rocks and gotten bruised, but we would have conceivably survived. Though the capsule seated six, there were only two of us aboard as it moved from the loading area toward the slope. I did not need to be reminded about the note on the window warning, in several languages, not to rock the capsule. Other than my heartbeat, the setting was very quiet as our bubble made its slow decline.

For a moment, I caught myself engrossed in the beauty of the experience. But then there was a slight jolt. The system had stopped, and we were stalled between two peaks that acted as a funnel for the wind to provide the capsule rocking that we were prohibited. There was no way to communicate with the outside world, so all we could do was dangle and hope for the best. After about a minute, we were moving again. In the distance an ascending capsule approached us on the parallel cable. Within moments we quietly passed each other like two spaceships making round trips to the moon.

Our capsule stopped briefly one more time before making its final descent. As it reached the landing, the door slid open and we quickly climbed out while the bubble continued its motion. I felt exhilarated.

Way above, Etna continued to gush smoke, but we were assured that was a good thing allowing the mountain to harmlessly let off steam. There was certainly no fear among the hundred or so adventurers waiting to get on board the gondolas for the ride up. Too bad the line was so long; I was ready to ride it again.

Back Street of Naples

Our group was walking through a back street of Naples on the way to a historic cemetery when the tour guide assured us that our destination was only about a kilometer away. We Americans are often illiterate about the metric system, but I knew that one kilometer was less than a mile but more than what I, who had been hobbled by a back sprain, was able to walk at that moment. So, as the group turned a corner, I huddled with the guide. She assured me that the group would be coming back along the same path and if I just sat in the small public square across the street I could rejoin when they returned in about forty-five minutes. That sounded good, though I was disappointed to be on the injured list.

There was nothing fancy about the square, just a few benches and chairs and a table. The block contained mostly shops where the clerks stood at the front entrances hoping for customers. In the distance, I could see the tour group walking away like troops on a mission. I on the other hand, sat on a bench hoping to absorb Italian life. Then something strange happened. I doubt if I had been seated two minutes when a man walked past me. His steps were very pronounced as though he was marching as his arms swayed. Most notable though was that he was whistling, quite nicely, not just any tune, but the "Triumphal March" from *Aida*.

Now, by my unofficial account, there are three cities in the world where that march, one of opera's most stirring, is most significant. They are, in ascending order, Cairo, where Giuseppe Verdi's masterpiece about an Ethiopian princess premiered in 1871; next is Milan, where the opera, with Verdi present, made its official debut in 1872 , but first is New Orleans, where since the 1880s the march, because of Carnival, has frequently been played between Twelfth Night and Mardi Gras as kings and queens have made their promenade on ballroom floors. My guess is that the march, through the centuries, has probably been played more in New Orleans than in any other city.

Not that there is anything unusual about an Italian whistling an opera, but the moment seemed too theatric to be true as though my character, listed as "The New Orleanian," took the stage and sat on a bench. Someone behind the curtain signaled to cue the whistler who then walked by while performing a professional rendition of the march. If there was an audience, it would have applauded. I just sat, perhaps too mesmerized by the moment, to respond.

Little did I know but that in the final scene something else strange was going to happen. . . .

That estimated forty-five minutes stretched past an hour. I, however, had not moved from my bench. I was fascinated by watching the locals, many of whom were shopkeepers, gather as the day wore on, joining in animated discussions. As the lone American, I was no doubt conspicuous. Then one of the shopkeepers, a friendly looking man wearing a tweed cap, broke from his conversation and approached me. He spoke in a broken English that was far superior to my broken Italian. Pointing down the street he said, "your group is coming back, it is about two blocks away." I thanked him and looked in the distance where I could see bobbing heads moving in my direction. I did wonder though, and still do, how he knew both that I was waiting for a group and where it was located at the moment. Maybe he had been standing outside his shop and overheard the initial conversation with the tour guide or maybe it was just the mystique of old Naples. Either way, I realize now that as I sat there alone in a strange city, he was watching out for me.

When I rejoined the tour group, I learned that it still had about another half-mile to its march which I endured, if not triumphally at least steadily. Those who had gone to the cemetery had stories to tell. Amazingly, though I just sat on a bench, so too did I.

Un Artista di New Orleans a Venezia

Tony Green knows how to pick his towns. The artist has apartments in two of the world's most poetic cities, Venice and New Orleans. In both places he has upstairs apartments in a quaint building in an old part of town; in Venice the neighborhood is what is still called the Jewish Ghetto; in New Orleans, the French Quarter. Great public squares are near; the Campo del Ghetto Nouveau and Jackson Square. Both places are reflected in his paintings.

We were early arriving for lunch at Upupa Ristorante located in his neighborhood. When we asked the guy at the bar if he could help us find Green's phone number he smiled, the number was on his speed dial. The reason was evident. His art decorates the walls.

When Green and his girlfriend Raffaella Toso arrived, he explained that while some people sing for their supper, at Upupa he paints for his meals.

Back in New Orleans, his art is also familiar including those murals on the walls at Rock'n'Bowl. His collection includes lush scenes of New Orleans street life and the pageantry of Venetian canals.

He is an enviably talented man who also plays the guitar. His music is jazz, that of his native town, but with a European flare known as "gypsy jazz." For Green, who was born in Naples but raised in New Orleans, his jazz idol is Django Reinhardt, a Belgian who he became fascinated with while studying art in that country. Green has appeared at the Jazz Fest in New Orleans, though he laments that his painting is leaving him less time for the music.

Green now spends nearly nine months a year in Venice but keeps up with his hometown. Our lunch conversation was peppered with questions of news from back home. Raffaella has accompanied him to New Orleans several times and says she especially enjoys seeing the Garden District.

A name like the "Jewish Ghetto" sounds a bit ominous though it is a totally peaceful and ecumenical neighborhood where everyone gets along. Crime is virtually nonexistent, particularly in a city of canals. "If someone robs a place," Raffaella explains, "they have to go get in line to wait for a water taxi."

Lunch was bountiful, as befits dining with someone that the staff sees as a friend more than a customer. After the meal, we walked to his apartment, which, like his apartment in New Orleans, has an open-air area where plants grow. Inside, the tables are those of an artist at work. Recently he has done a series of New Orleans second line parades.

Then we did our own second line—minus the music, handkerchiefs, police escort, and dancing: At a nearby bar, we peeked inside to see one of Green's paintings of a New Orleans musician. When we took a picture Green teased to the bartender, "paparazzi."

During some parts of the year, the narrow street that leads to a water taxi stop is underwater. This day, the Grand Canal was tame, and the street was filled with vendors as though they had arisen from the sea.

Our visit ended where most visits in Venice start and finish—waiting for a boat. As the taxi puttered away, I glanced at Tony and Raffaella who stood at the edge of the canal framed by centuries old buildings. They looked like a scene from one of his paintings. Considering the English to Italian translation, it must be good to be Tony Green; even better to be Antonio Verdi.

Mussolini, A Margherita Pizza, and George Clooney

A tour guide at the back of the boat was pointing to some of the sites as the craft raced toward Bellagio (The real village, not the hotel in Vegas.). Italy's lake region is one of the most picturesque spots in a country already stunning with beauty both designed by nature and by ancient architects.

Lake Como's shore is rich with stories of kings, saints, artists, and even Benito Mussolini who was gunned down nearby. Sometimes history can be mindboggling, especially when its characters flow as quickly as a motorboat, but there was one name that gave a rise to all the passengers. "See that building," the guide, Mariana, said as she pointed toward the shore at a chateau, "that's where George Clooney stays." There was a gasp worthy of Michelangelo. Soon the visitors were overwhelmed by another historic landmark, a restaurant where Clooney sometimes ate.

I have been thinking about Italy since it was first hit hard by *the* virus. As a united country, Italy is younger than the United States, having been consolidated into a nation in 1861. As a peninsula, the land is ancient. Its pre-Clooney history includes one of history's all-time famous disasters at Pompeii but also global importance: The Roman Empire shaped Western civilization.

For the pathos of the moment, I am reminded of the little things—the small towns where old men gather at the town squares each evening for animated discussions; nearby, boys kick a soccer ball. There are fountains and ancient churches whose belfries acknowledge each new hour. From the cafes there is the smell of frying garlic, anise, and olive oil. At the bars, the tourists sip limoncello while the locals have another Moretti beer.

I was once in Italy on an Easter Sunday in a town, Pienza, whose cathedral was commissioned by an early Pope, Pius II (1458-1464). Pius frequently stayed in an adjacent palace he designed to be his retreat. This, I thought, was going to be quite an experience, Easter Sunday in Italy at a church that a pope built. The church was packed, as expected for that day, but what surprised was that there was no support staff except for one usher. During the Mass, the usher also did what an altar boy does helping the priest, including holding the plate beneath the chalice during Communion. There was no choir, so Easter was a two man show.

There was one parable though: Our group was running a little late, so there was no space left in the pews. The usher directed me to a chair that had been set up near the altar. For my tardiness I had the best seat in the house. Or, to quote Matthew, "The last shall be first."

Food is always part of the discussion when Italy is the topic, including the story that in 1889 Queen Margherita of Savoy, wife of Italian King Umberto, visited Naples. To honor her, a local pizzeria operator, Raffaele Esposito, created a pizza topped with the colors of the Italian flag; mozzarella for white; basil for green and tomatoes for red. He named it Pizza Margherita. Those ingredients had probably been used on pizza bread before, but never with a name. From that day, the Margherita became famous, and so did the pizza business.

Dean Martin's song "That's Amore" is about love and contains the line "When the moon hits your eye like a big pizza pie, that's amore."

May the moon be bright over Lake Como. And may joy itself soon move from last to first.

Making it Past Winter

Fiorina, our tour guide, was herself a Greek classic whose native good looks were worthy of a statue and could have made her a movie star. Throughout the afternoon, she led us around her island showing the villages, hills, town squares and panoramic views that are part of a tour guide's daily odyssey.

What could not be seen, but certainly felt, are ancient gods that traverse the hills, given immortality by epic legends. (Off the coast of one island there is a rock that looks like the bow of a ship pointed upward. Legend has it that was Ulysses's boat that had been turned to stone.) Listen carefully and the sirens are singing, whether you can hear them or not.

Fiorina's stage is her island, and she delivers her lines with good English embellished by enough accent to complement her Greek look. She was articulate and well informed—and spoke passionately about her island.
Then came *the* question,

It was a question that probably all of us on the tour, myself included, had wanted to ask, but were not sure if we should, as though it might anger the gods. That did not stop one woman in the group, who within earshot of the all-knowing Zeus asked, "What about the economy?"

For the first time that afternoon, Fiorina seemed to struggle for words. At the time, Greece's troubled finances had been Europe's anvil, plunging the continent toward the sharks. Fiorina paused, took a swig of water and then seemed to undergo a catharsis. Her mind, associated with a people who produced some of the world's greatest philosophy, raced for an answer and landed at "frankness." Here was her moment of releasing the frustration. "Honestly," she told the group,"I don't see how we are going to make it past winter."

Then she revealed that her dad, a retired government worker, just saw his pension slashed by six hundred euros per month. She wondered if she would have to provide more support for her family, though the crisis was causing a decline in tourism, her industry. She lamented that she had believed in the various government officials that she had voted for, but nothing had worked. Then came her diatribe about the euro, drachmas, and the European Union. "It is like having one dress," she said of the latter "and trying to make it fit three different people. Greece is different from the other places." She also attacked the stereotypes: "We are not lazy Greeks, we work hard."

I felt sorry for Fiorina. At another time in another place her looks, charm, and intelligence could place her on top of the world, but her world is an island—a relatively small one at that.

Though we could not totally feel her pain, I doubt if any of the Americans, myself included, felt the same pessimism. We, after all, come from the land of the bailout where a strong central government would never let a state roll over and die. Certainly, former nemesis Germany and the European powerhouses will keep Greece afloat. An island that gave the world moussaka and Socrates must be preserved.

Fiorina (that's not her real name) would express none of that optimism, at least not this moment.

Later that evening, the cruise ship glided from the island. The sunset had turned the Mediterranean coast gold. It was the end of another beautiful day in Greece, though even sirens sometimes sing the blues.

Helga of Prague

One day Helga was leading a tour group near the Czech Republic's Parliament building in downtown Prague. Traffic had stopped because of a small fire in one of the adjacent buildings. Approaching a fireman, Helga asked, "Was our president in the fire?" The fireman smiled faintly and replied, "You're going to have to pray a lot harder for that to happen!"

Simple as that story is, it is loaded with significance. Helga was in her mid-fifties which means that for much of her life she has lived behind the Iron Curtain where mere citizens never ridiculed government officials in public, particularly to men in uniform. Secondly, the reason she disliked President Miloš Zeman, a converted former Communist who is the country's first popularly elected chief executive (His immediate predecessors were selected by Parliament), is not because of doctrine or persecution but because he smokes—incessantly. He smokes when appearing in public, he smokes when addressing Parliament. "He is disgusting," Helga said. To Helga, the lungs are more important than Lenin. As we toured, I saw many old buildings where kings, tyrants, and composers visited. History is displayed in many layers. Nevertheless, despite the many grand art works, I most enjoyed watching the locals discover themselves. At one point, Helga wanted to show us a garden in a Parliament courtyard. She asked a policeman who politely explained that our group could not enter because Parliament was in session. Nevertheless, Helga was thrilled: "A few years ago I could have never asked a policeman a question," she said, "and if I did, he would not have answered."

In case there is any doubt who won between capitalism and Communism, one of the downtown businesses is a capitalist showcase—The Museum of Communism. For an admission, visitors can see displays about the bad old days, including the disregard for environment—the Reds never thought green. The museum is contained in a former palace that now contains a casino and across the alley from the museum's entrance is a McDonald's.

Most of the world knows Good King Wenceslas from the carol. In Prague the king's towering statue is venerated as the site of the 1989 protests that were the beginning of the end of Communism. Václav Havel, the first post-Communist president, who was a philosopher and a poet as well as a revolutionary, is very much of a beloved figure in the Czech Republic, but here too Helga, the liberated social commentator that she is, was critical of him—"Perhaps he did not fully understand government."

European history is so filled with wars and upheavals that one is hesitant to feel too optimistic, but it is noteworthy that the people move freely between countries as the Iron Curtain has been ripped to shreds. At the Czech/German border, a tour guide pointed to dreary looking buildings off to the side. Once they headquartered border control operations; now they are empty, a victim to the conquest of liberty.

Today, Helga still leads her tours and is no doubt giving her opinions. I should point out that Helga is not her real name, but that is my choice. Peace has broken out, but there is always someone who might not have gotten the message.

Election Day in Liverpool

We just happened to be in Liverpool on the same day that the British were holding a national election. I thought it would be interesting to observe how one of the world's other great democracies performs on voting day.

I had expected to see trucks with loudspeakers and campaign workers handing out leaflets from key intersections, but there was none of that. British elections are different from ours in several ways, including:

By law there can be no public electioneering on Election Day.
Voting is on a Thursday with the polling hours spread from 7:00 a.m. to 10:00 p.m.
Emphasis is on the party rather than the candidates and there are more political
parties to vote for.

Other than one sign pointing to a voting poll, there was no indication that anything special was happening that day, but oh, something else was:

By around 9:30 that morning we noticed clusters of people gathered around a couple of microphones located downtown. Our tour guide explained that they were not there for demonstrations or politics, but, far more importantly, especially in Liverpool—to sing.

Even more significant than having been in Liverpool on national Election Day was to have been there during the week of the celebration of the fiftieth anniversary of the Beatles' recording of the brilliant *Sergeant Pepper* album. Each morning that week, one song, with the help of a local radio station, was featured at 10:30 a.m. There would be a citywide singalong. To the rest of Great Britain, it was Election Day; to the people of Liverpool it was "When I'm Sixty-Four" Day. Right on the hour, the bus driver parked his vehicle and turned the radio loud. A fast-talking Cockney accented DJ prompted the town to start singing:

When I get older losing my hair,
Many years from now.
Will you still be sending me a Valentine . . .

At intervals, the broadcast would switch to one of the street groups, though we could barely hear them because of our singing in the bus. No stone-faced king or gallant warrior staring down from a pedestal was as important to the town's history as the four native boys whose music spread across the world as no empire could.

Statues of John, Paul, George, and Ringo walking together, in the direction of America, embellish the Mersey River waterfront where the ferry that crosses the river is painted psychedelic.

Around 5:00 that afternoon, the tour guide noticed a traffic build up and suggested that the night might be especially busy as folks gathered in pubs for the election returns. So that was the answer. To see Election Day politics in Great Britain go to the pubs, but there is little action until after 10:00 p.m.when the votes come in.

That night British politics was atwitter as the ruling Conservative party did far worse than expected, creating a badly divided government. The big issues of the day would be even more contentious.

Of course, as the "Four Boys" knew, politics would not be necessary if everyone lived in a yellow submarine.

Joan of Arc's Teardrops

In the old town section of the French city of Rouen, there is a shop called Chocolaterie Auzou Rouen "Gros Horloge" that masterfully prepares classic sweets. In addition to its macaroons, its most famous product is bolstered by legend as well as taste. It is chocolate covered almonds known as "Joan of Arc Teardrops." (Given what she went through her teardrops could have justifiably been almond sized.) The relevance is that the shop is near the site where Joan, to be known as the Maid of Orleans and later canonized as a saint, was burned at the stake.

Her statue which stands in the French Quarter is a striking image; this young girl, an eternal symbol of youth, dressed as a knight, performing as a general in the face of adversity, her extended right arm elevating a flag as though to charge into the future.

We needed Joan to inspire us back in 2005 as we picked up the pieces from the Storm and our lives.

By coincidence, I spent a morning in Rouen during that time. It was there that her adventure came to an end. According to legend, her being disguised as a boy gave prosecutors all the argument they needed to declare her to be a witch and to face the punishment.

Her fate was met at the Place du Vieux Marché, a town square where the stake was placed in the center. Today, there is a garden on the fatal site with a small monument marking the spot. At the front of the garden is a church, L'église Sainte-Jeanne-d'Arc, which in this old city of medieval buildings is surprisingly modern. The roof, instead of being guarded by gargoyles and marble saints, swoops up to represent flames angling toward heaven. Leave it to Joan, stirring things up again.

Old town Rouen is a busy area filled with quaint shops, cafes, and omnipresent selfie-taking tourists, just like in old town New Orleans, named after the French city of Joan's conquest.

Joan has been good for business. Historically, she has also been good for inspiration.

When teardrops are chocolate almonds, the world must be a better place.

Bouncing to St. Barth

When the trip was planned, I had no idea that the Saints would even make the playoffs, much less be hosting a home game. But airfares were paid, reservations were made so the trip, in January '07, went on.

My strategy was that once we arrived at the Guanahani Resort on the French Caribbean Island of St. Barth I would make a dash to the bar where there would certainly be a widescreen TV showing the game. Now, I do not usually approve of televisions in bars, especially at resorts. Unfortunately, the Guanahani bar would have met my approval on every night except this one. Not only was there no TV, but no inkling that the French-speaking bartender and patrons were even aware of the game. The truth hurt: there were people on this continent who did not know that the Saints were playing the Eagles.

That realization was a disappointment, but by that time I was just grateful to be on land. Only an hour earlier I had experienced what remains as my all-time worst travel experience.

It all began when the American Airlines jet descended on the neighboring island of St. Martin where the international airport is. There were storm clouds all around the plane as it glided toward land. Once in the airport, we learned that the shuttle flight to St. Barth on an island-hopping plane service called Caribe Air had been cancelled. Ours was to be the last flight of the day, so our trip was beginning by being stranded on the wrong island without reservations.

Someone mentioned, though, that there would be a night ferry leaving to St. Barth from the town of Marigot. We hurried and took an expensive half-hour taxi ride to the Marigot port. The ferry tickets were not cheap either, about eighty dollars a piece and I had already taken a loss from the Caribe Air fare that I was not sure if I would ever get back.

There was nothing fancy about the ferry that looked like a workboat with a passenger area. The seating was on large plastic cubes. A bar was the only amenity. It was depicted in a brochure showing happy passengers sipping rum drinks while a native bartender smiled broadly. I promised myself to be like those passengers once the crossing started.

I was seated facing the stern in such a way that I could see the island of St. Martin fade away as the ship moved toward the sea. Once the ship passed the breakwater, however, a strange thing happened to the St. Martin coastline; it started moving up and down. The foul weather that had caused the Caribe Air flight to be cancelled was now angering the Caribbean. For more than an hour during this night, made even darker by a canopy of black clouds, the ferry would buck, shake, pitch, jump, dive, guffaw (not really), wobble, and weave.

There was no assuring voice from the pilothouse telling us that we were experiencing a few minutes of turbulence and that things would be better soon, nor were there life jackets in view. The bartender did manage to stagger across the deck making deliveries to the passengers. It wasn't drinks he was giving out, but barf bags. For the rest of the trip, my fellow cruisers would be leaning over coughing into the bags while the boat bounced over the waves. This, I thought, while listening to the wretched symphony of those around me, is the worst travel experience of my life.

Once we neared the St. Barth town of Gustav where its harbor calmed the sea our agony lessened. We were a shaken bunch. A van ride down a bumpy road to the Guanahani was smooth by comparison, but now there was the Saints issue to contend with.

With the bar having failed us, we went back to our cottage where there was a fancy satellite TV that I could not work. A French speaking staff member came, pushed a few buttons, and could not understand our excitement when the first station to appear was one from Philadelphia about to the show the Saints game.

From room service came cheeseburgers and beers. The night that had begun so terribly ended so happily—the Saints won.

Outside, a rushing patch of clouds was starting to darken the sky again. Weather changes quickly in the Caribbean—and so too do experiences.

WAR

Fighting on the Beaches

Some kids were playing on Omaha Beach, building sandcastles. Nearby an adult couple walked along the sand at shore's edge, presumably looking for shells, the nautical kind rather than those fired from cannons. The shards of war have long been taken from this historic beach, now it stands as it should—a quiet passive place where castles are built, if only for the moment.

If the day is clear, the faint coastline of Britain across the Channel can be seen. If the imagination is even clearer it can envision two thousand ships as they approached on June 6, 1944. The mind peppers the sky with hundreds of bombers heading over France that day.

Nearby is the town of Arromanches. It was there that one of two artificial piers was built to unload the Allied ships as they approached the beach. The town itself now survives on D-Day tourism, including a museum, shops and, at least on the day we were there, a character dressed to imitate Winston Churchill. Two of the best quotes from the war were due to the British Prime Mister. One contained the fiery words of his rallying speech to Parliament:

> We shall defend our island, whatever the cost may be. We shall fight on the beaches, we shall fight on the landing grounds, we shall fight in the fields and in the streets, we shall fight in the hills; we shall never surrender.

And the other great quote is about Churchill rather than by him. It is attributed to American broadcaster Edward R. Murrow who, in speaking of the impact of Churchill's speeches said, "He mobilized the English language and sent it to battle."

In Churchill's day, fighting on the beaches was made more successful by a New Orleans-made vessel: Andrew Higgins's landing boats were constructed in the city. They are what brought the troops from the transport ships to near the beaches where they could indeed fight on the landing grounds. Hitler knew about New Orleanian Higgins and referred to him as "the New Noah." Years later, historian Steven Ambrose would claim that Allied Commander Dwight Eisenhower once referred to Higgins as the man who won the war. Higgins wasn't alone in deserving that praise, but it is true that the landing crafts that were key to the greatest invasion in history were first tested on Lake Pontchartrain.

As fortune would have it, Ambrose's academic trail eventually took him to the University of New Orleans where he excelled as a leading authority on the war. By 1994, at the time of the invasion's fiftieth anniversary, Ambrose was one of the experts seen on just about every war documentary. For the fiftieth anniversary of D-Day, he led a group of tourists to Omaha Beach where he was so moved by being there that historian Doug Brinkley would recall the professor leading the charge toward the shore. Ambrose was in charge that day, Brinkley would recall, he was Eisenhower.

Ambrose's book, *Band of Brothers,* is a major contribution to the war's history, especially after it was made into a TV series by HBO, (I have watched some episodes so many times that I can almost recite them, except for those shows when I felt too emotionally wrenched that I couldn't watch more.) Ambrose led another charge while in New Orleans and that was to build a museum dedicated to the war. In a city of attractions, the National World War II Museum, where the site includes a former Higgins plant, is as triumphant as American soldiers marching through the streets of Paris.

General Colin Powell once said of America's wars "that the only land we ever asked for was enough land to bury our dead." The grandest of such spots is the Normandy American Cemetery and Memorial located on a Normandy bluff overlooking the charging sea. Battalions of wooden crosses and Stars of David are the sentinels along the Atlantic Coast.

Normandy always leaves me wanting to know more. Once I was on a cruise ship moving along the British side of the English Channel. From a map on a TV monitor, I could tell that on the opposite side was Normandy, but I was not sure of exactly what location. The night was solid black. I was mesmerized by the darkness thinking what the moment must have been like to a nineteen-year-old soldier sailing through the darkness not knowing what the next day would bring for him or even if he would live to see the day after. Then I noticed something from the Normandy side, a blinking light, possibly from a lighthouse. In another era it could have been a sign from the European mainland pleading to be liberated.

On a summer night, a navy of Noahs was heading its way.

St. Crispin's Day—The New Orleans Connection

October 25 is St. Crispin's Day. The Feast, named in honor of a third-century martyred saint, would be obscure had it not been that the 1415 Battle of Agincourt, matching the forces of King Henry V of England versus the French, was fought on that date. In one of history's great upsets, Henry's outnumbered army won partially because of this successful use of new-fangled weapons called longbows.

In another example of that domino effect by which history works, from that setting something would evolve out of New Orleans centuries later that would today have a positive economic impact throughout Northern Europe.

Here's what happened:

Agincourt itself might have been forgotten as just another one of many European battles with the French and the English pounding each other, except that in approximately 1599 one of the most famous of all Englishmen, William Shakespeare (or whomever wrote under that name) wrote a play called *Henry V.* In the drama, the warrior King Harry (as he was known to his pals) addresses his army the night before the battle. Shakespeare's words were a moving soliloquy as Harry tells his troops that tomorrow, the day of the battle, is St. Crispin's Day and that those who fight and survive will forever be remembered by that day.

This being Shakespeare there are many great lines in the speech but one that would reverberate in New Orleans comes near the end:

> But we in it shall be remembered—We few, we happy few, we band of brothers;
> for he today that sheds his blood with me shall be my brother; be he ne'er so vile

Now the scene shifts to the New Orleans area, where in 2001 historian Stephen Ambrose published a book about a US Army unit known as "Easy Company," a part of the 506th Airborne Division. The book traced the group from basic training through D-Day and across Northern Europe into Germany and Hitler's Eagle's Nest. Borrowing from King Harry via Shakespeare, Ambrose called his book, *Band of Brothers.* The story was so compelling that HBO made it into a mini-series, itself a masterpiece.

A few years ago, I took a tour of Normandy and then into Holland, Luxembourg, Belgium, and Germany—the places where the fighting was hard. During the tour, episodes of *Band of Brothers* were played on the bus's TV system. Historic markers along the way referred to scenes from *Band of Brothers.* Tourists were snapping pictures of sites they were familiar with because of the book. Much has been written about the Allied invasion of Europe. Cornelius Ryan's 1959 masterpiece *The Longest Day,* which was made into a popular movie in '62, was the early most important effort. Now the bible is *Band of Brothers.* Each year tourists invade the beaches not for sun but for solace. For many, their inspiration is a book from New Orleans with a title inspired by an ancient battle fought on St. Crispin's Day.

Unrealized by many of those visitors is that Agincourt, the battle site, is not far from where they are. It is near the Pas-De-Calais, famous because it is the shortest point across the English Channel and the spot where the Allies duped the Nazis into thinking they would arrive. Agincourt goes down in history as an unusual battle. It was originally studied for its weaponry; now it is remembered for its words.

The Angel of Bastogne

In the Belgian town of Bastogne there is a Chinese restaurant named Cite Wok located near the town square. At first glance it looks pretty much like any buffet place anywhere in the world, except for a plaque outside. Bastogne is an ancient city, but its most talked about history traces back to Christmas Eve of 1944, as does the writing on the plaque.

At that site there was a military aid station to which some of the wounded from the battles were evacuated, most on a stretcher attached to a Jeep. During the evening of December 24, 1944, the writing on the plaque reports, "Over thirty US wounded and 1 volunteer Belgian nurse (Renee LeMaire) were instantly killed by a German Bomb."

There is an episode in the HBO series *Band of Brothers* based on LeMaire who is now remembered as "The Angel of Bastogne." In the film she befriended an Army medic from Louisiana. They shared the French language and war stories. On the day after the bombing, the medic drove to the aid station and found it in shambles. Within the rubble he found her headscarf.

My father was a medic. He was from rural Louisiana. He spoke French. In later life he would also frequently speak of Bastogne. I would like to believe that he visited that aid station and that he had met Lemaire. The two would have quickly compared their Louisiana French with the Belgian dialect. He would have been one of thousands of young men trapped in the Ardennes Forest during one of the coldest winters on record.

He loved the holidays especially when he could look back at the Christmas of '44 from a distance. Bastogne was critical to the battle because it was a crossroads town; whoever controlled it controlled the roads to the port at Antwerp.

Bastogne would also be the setting of one of the war's most celebrated stories: An American combat unit, the 101 Airborne, was headquartered at a Belgian Army base in town. At the battle's worst moment, Bastogne was totally surrounded by the German Army. An envoy was sent by the German general asking US General Anthony McAuliffe to surrender. Hearing the demand, McAuliffe muttered to himself, "Nuts!" Told by his subordinates that he would have to issue a formal reply, McAuliffe searched for words. One of his aides suggested his earlier statement. And so it was, the word "Nuts!" was sent back to the German general. Fortunately for posterity's sake, an American war correspondent heard the reply and reported it back home as a brash statement of defiance.

For days the situation was bleak but then the fog lifted. American planes were able to drop supplies. A tank force commanded by General George Patton broke through the enemy encirclement. Back home McAuliffe's response made headlines across the country. Today, near the room where McAuliffe made his reply there are pictures from the war including one showing a US Jeep bringing "Pere Noel" to visit Bastogne,

In today's Bastogne, the town center, now known as McAuliffe Square, is surrounded, not by Nazi tanks, but ice cream shops and cafes. A bust of the general overlooks the festivity.

Most tourists are oblivious to the plaque outside nearby Cite Wok. They don't know that at that site on Christmas Eve, 1944, Bastogne got its own angel.

Renee LaMaire probably treated and made the acquaintance of many American troops. I would later learn that the medic referred to in the film was not my father but Eugene Roe, a paratrooper/medic from Bayou Chene, Louisiana who was part of Easy Company, the group depicted in *Band of Brothers*. For my father, the war would end in Belgium where he was hospitalized for severe frost bite. For Roe, the war and its aftermath would continue including treating liberated concentration camp victims.

Both men would return to Louisiana where they had been raised, probably no more than sixty miles apart.

Their lives were enriched by having perhaps known Renee LaMaire. In the unpredictable ways of their war, the crossroads truly led through Bastogne.

Riding Hitler's Elevator

On my list of favorite things to do, riding in a crowded elevator ranks somewhere below getting root canal surgery. Add to the situation that to get to the elevator you have to walk through a long damp tunnel and then wait in front of the elevator door in anticipation of a reported forty or so fellow riders being packed in for a 124-meter (roughly four hundred feet) trip up a tube in a mountain peak. The situation is made even more ominous with the knowledge that the elevator was built for and used by Adolph Hitler. At that point the anticipation of the experience, at least for the phobic among us, reaches the colonoscopy level. (Hitler might have been squeamish too, supposedly he was claustrophobic and had vertigo. He did not go to the top very often, though Eva seemed to enjoy it.)

Our schedule that afternoon in the Bavarian Alps was to visit Hitler's *Kehlsteinhaus*, or as the Americans called it, "the Eagle's Nest." Not that he was trying to suck up to the *Führer* or anything, but the mountain peak retreat was built at the behest of Martin Bormann, Hitler's private secretary, who used Nazi party money to build the getaway as a present to Hitler for his fiftieth birthday.

Hitler's gal, Eva Braun, was reportedly especially fond of romping in the celestial cottage where she could marvel at the valleys below and the Austrian Alps in the distance. In one room is a marble fireplace mantel given to Hitler by his good friend Benito Mussolini, perhaps in anticipation of the years of glory they would share.

In the days immediately after the war, American and French troops rushed to the place in sort of a grown version of the king of the mountain game. Mussolini's fireplace was left pockmarked from chips taken away by conquering soldiers.

Tourism was the ultimate conqueror. The Bavarian government laid claim to the place where a trip to the top in the beautifully appointed brass elevator opens to a restaurant, gift shops, some pictures from the Reich days and spectacular views.

First though, there is the issue of getting to the top. There must have been two hundred people lined up in the tunnel with the line nudging a little closer each time the elevator door opened having released its previous load. When our turn came, my strategy was to try to stand next to the elevator operator, which somehow seemed a bit more assuring. I watched gloomily as others entered in anticipation of the full load: two, three, four. I wished those in line would somehow go away. And then a miracle: With only seven of us in the elevator and another man about to enter, the operator put up the palm of his hand to tell him not to. The man had paused to take a picture which was verboten. To make his point, the operator closed the door and began our journey—seven of us in an elevator built for forty. I was thrilled. Had they been around, there would have been enough extra room for Adolph and Eva. She might have needed to hold his hand.

Writing Home

On July 4, 1944, a soldier in the American Army, camped out somewhere in France, had written to his sister:

"I'm sure you've heard and seen much about the invasion since D-Day," the soldier, my father, Ellis Laborde wrote to his sister, Lena. "I did not arrive in France on D-Day but I came in shortly afterward, and there was still much to be seen, and plenty hard fighting to do," he continued. "I was in action several times since. Thank God thus far I didn't even get a scratch."

Wartime mail was heavily censored for fear that if somehow seized by the enemy the letters could give valuable information. Soldiers were not allowed to be specific about their locations or casualties they witnessed. Though they must have been bursting with feelings about the hell they had lived through and the triumph they had experienced, the letters were forced to be subdued, more about the setting than the fighting: "At first the Frenchmen were rather cold towards us," he wrote. "The welcome we received here was nothing like it had been in Sicily."

For the rest of his life, Sicily would be what all else was measured against. He was a medic, and while under fire during the invasion of Sicily, my dad rushed to save a wounded soldier. A passing general saw the action, thought it heroic, and later issued him a certificate of commendation. Years later he would learn that he had also been awarded a Bronze Star Medal. Sicily was also the site of one of the war's lighter moments. One day after the fighting was over, a wealthy local man drove into the camp and asked to see the commanding officer. The man had connections in Louisiana and wanted to entertain any soldiers from there. That evening the Louisianians in the group were served a full pasta dinner at the man's villa.

France was different: "Their attitude is gradually changing," my father wrote of the locals, "now that they are finding out what the Germans said about us was just plain ole German propaganda."

Optimism was high in the summer of '44. With the Allies having broken through, the war in Europe seemed nearly over—maybe within a month or so. Earlier in his letter the soldier had speculated about what he might do after the war—perhaps landing a job with Public Service, New Orleans' utility company at the time, or going back to his previous job at a hotel, or, maybe—he joked—just retiring.

As happy as that July Fourth seemed to be, his favorite holiday, Christmas, would that year be miserable. Rather than surrender what was by then a hopeless cause, the Nazis made a determined last stand near the German border. This final great confrontation of the European war, to be known as The Battle of the Bulge, was fought during one of the area's coldest winters ever. Soldiers, topped by layers of snow, shivered in foxholes. The "scratch" that he had thus far avoided at the time of his Fourth of July letter came in a painful way––a leg so frostbitten that it almost had to be amputated. The leg was saved but for the rest of his life he suffered with it.

In the summer of '44, though, his most serious malady had been sheer loneliness: "Please pass this short letter around so the rest of the family can read it as well," he concluded. "A letter a week from you would be highly appreciated. Certainly you will not let me down, will you?"

He was in a hospital in Belgium when the war ended. The news was echoed by a distant bugler playing the "Star-Spangled Banner." That would be the sweetest message delivered on either side of the Atlantic.

In Search of General Rose

It happened late one night. I was sitting at home literally stunned and shocked by what I had just read. Until that moment, I hadn't known how the story had ended. I wondered if my father had known. If he did, he never said so. I'll never know for sure.

I was raised hearing war stories as told by my father, an old solider who was in the thick of it during the Big One in Europe. As a medic, he was part of the invasion force that swept Sicily. He was also there on the beaches at Normandy and part of the movement north that took him into Belgium near the German border and the snow-packed fields of the Bulge. His military service ended in a hospital where he almost lost a leg from being holed up in a foxhole during the war's deepest freeze.

Among the many stories was one that took place in Sicily. One day he was attending to a wounded soldier while under heavy fire. A Jeep drove up carrying some officers, one of whom asked, "Hey soldier do you know what you're doing?" As my father told the story, he nodded while muttering to himself something like, "Why don't you come and help?" Instead, the Jeep moved on.

Several days later, my father was called into the office of the company commander where he was handed a sheet of paper with a message punched out on a field typewriter. Among its accolades it stated that: "While riding in a column of vehicles near Campobello, Sicily, that was being bombed and strafed by the enemy, you exposed yourself with utter disregard for your own safety in order to care for a wounded soldier." The letter of commendation was signed by the ranking officer from the Jeep who turned out to be Brigadier General Maurice Rose.

General Rose was a big name in our household. I've thought about him just as I have wondered how close the bombing and strafing came to my never existing.

Rose was not one of the legendary generals from the war, so I was surprised and impressed that evening when I was reading Stephen Ambrose's book, *Citizen Soldier: The US Army From the Normandy Beaches to the Bulge to the Surrender of Germany.* In telling about the frozen Christmas warfare at the Bulge, Ambrose makes reference to, "Maj. Gen Maurice Rose, the much-admired and much loved CO of the Third Armored." I was pleased—as though a member of the family had been canonized—his reputation chiseled into military history for being loved and admired.

That was the first reference to Rose in the book, the other one came toward the end. I was close enough to being finished that I stayed up a little later reading when out of the camouflage of words and paragraphs, Ambrose fired a cannon:

Once again General Rose was in a Jeep. This time he was leading a column attacking a German tank training center. Turning a corner, his driver ran into the rear of an enemy tank. The German tank commander, estimated to be about eighteen years old, opened his turret hatch and leveled his gun at the general, yelling at him to surrender.

Gesturing at Rose's pistol at his side, the tank commander, who seemed extremely agitated, kept yelling. As Ambrose tells it: "Rose lowered his right arm to release his web belt and thus drop the hip holster to the ground. Apparently, the German boy thought he was going to draw his pistol; in a screaming rage, he fired his machine pistol straight into Rose's head, killing him instantly."

Maurice Rose was the first and only division commander killed in the European Theater.

That's when I was stunned. General Rose—another victim of the war. That wasn't supposed to happen. I had this momentary sinking feeling. I hadn't realized how much the man affected me.

There was something else I didn't know: Ambrose wrote that it was later rumored in the American Army that the German who shot the general did so because, "he knew Rose was Jewish." Ambrose, however, dismisses that theory. The gunner, in a chance meeting, could have hardly known that.

Rose died March 31, 1945, less than two months before the war in Europe ended. What a waste. The teenage soldier who killed him might have gone on to live a long life. He would have seen his ravaged country rebuilt, divided, and reunited. Did the moment when he killed a great man haunt him? Or had it been blotted out in the mind of a kid pushed into combat by a wicked government in the last desperate days of the war?

A website for the Third Armored Division has a bio about the general which says that he was so brusque with the Germans in negotiating their surrender in Tunisia that he was nicknamed, "Old Gravel Face." After his death, the *New York Times* eulogized that the American Army had been, "deprived of one of its most skilled and gallant officers and a man of rare personal charm." His many awards, having fought in both world wars, included the Legion of Honor given by the French Army.

There is another award to this story. Many years after the war my father heard from a friend that veterans could write to the US Defense Department to get any medals they might have earned but that during the postwar turmoil had been overlooked. From Washington came the expected Purple Heart, plus something unexpected–a Bronze Star Medal for bravery. It was a distant salute from General Rose.

A Plane Named *Enola Gay*

Except for the few people gathered around him, there seemed nothing special about the old man seated at a table in the cavernous Morial Convention Center hall. To those who bothered to ask him questions, he gave the answers that he had given hundreds of times, but the enormity of the hall and the toll of age reduced him that day to just another old solider with memories.

Of all the old soldiers, the million or so who saw action during World War II, no one's story would have quite the exclamation point as the old man's, whose memories took him to when he was a dashing young pilot, one of the Army Air Corps's best. On August 6, 1945, he was at the controls of the B-29 bomber that he named after his mother, Enola Gay, steering it over the Pacific to drop an atomic bomb on the Japanese city of Hiroshima.

For the rest of his life, Paul Tibbets, who died in 2007, would say proudly that he has never lost sleep over his mission. He had not felt guilt or doubts about bringing the bomb to Japan despite the enormity of its damage.

Had the bomb not been dropped, the war would have continued. Battalions of American and British soldiers, relieved that they had survived the combat in Europe, where the war ended three months earlier, faced the possibility of being shipped to the Pacific to die in an invasion of Japan.

That Japan was already a physically defeated nation made no difference. In Germany, where not even his strongest supporters confused Adolph Hitler with being a god, the generals, in the waning days of the war, sacrificed their nation's young rather than concede defeat. In Japan, where the emperor *was* linked to a deity, crazed men preferred to see their people perish than for their people to see them lose. Sitting on the stumps of bombed out Europe, American boys, to whom Japan was another planet, were nervous at the prospects of going there. US Marines and sailors, already in bloody combat throughout the Pacific islands, knew how brutal the relentless Japanese could be.

Tibbets was in New Orleans for the opening of the Pacific Wing at the National D-Day Museum in 2001.

Historian Stephen Ambrose made the museum possible. Like the GIs at the Battle of the Bulge, Ambrose's last battle was his toughest. Only there would be no General Patton riding in to rescue him from his lung cancer.

During his final days, Ambrose wrote a very special book, *To America: Personal Reflections of an Historian,* about his career. The *Enola Gay's* bomb was the first of two to fall on Japan. Three days later, after the Japanese still had not surrendered, a different flight dropped its load on Nagasaki. In one section of his book, Ambrose told candidly about his shifting attitudes toward the bombings:

> Truman's critics, including me, charged that . . . the bomb was the first act of the Cold War rather than the last act of World War II. Truman used the bomb not so much to force a Japanese surrender but to show the Russians that we are not afraid to use it. We critics also believed that the potential American casualty figures were grossly inflated. . . .
>
> Here is what I learned since. The Japanese government was by no means ready to surrender. There were logical, sensible people in Japan, but they were not allowed a say in decision making. . . . The need to end the war was overwhelming. The Japanese were starving and killing American POWs, mainly fliers who had been shot down over Japan. Meanwhile thousands or more civilians in the Japan-

held territories in Asia and the offshore islands were dying every day because of Japanese mistreatment. So today, I tell my students. Thank God for Harry Truman. For his courage and decisiveness.

I asked Tibbets if his plane had experienced any shock waves from the blast. He said it did. The real shock waves, of course, were felt around the world: horror and grief in some places, unbridled joy in others. The American soldiers abroad, now given a chance to live a full life rather than to die on a Japanese beach, would be heading toward New York and San Diego rather than Tokyo. The brash, cocky, expansive, booming days of postwar America were beginning.

Those days got a jump start because of the *Enola Gay.* Each anniversary of the war's end becomes increasingly important as there are even fewer old soldiers left.

For those who have survived, may they, like Paul Tibbets did for so long, sleep well tonight.

FINAL WORD: GESUNDHEIT!

The Sneeze

April is a big month for sneezing, such as recently when I was climbing the steps of a building that was surrounded by flora. First there was the tickling in my eyes, followed by three rapid-fire blasts. There was a pause and then another sneeze. "That's four" a man climbing the steps behind me said. "Jeez, he's actually counting my sneezes," I thought to myself as the fifth one burst loose. I made a point of containing myself until he had passed me and was inside the building. He would never know that there had been a sixth.

That incident reminded me of the afternoon a couple of springs ago when, as I was driving up to my home, I could feel something building between the eyes and the nose and knew it was going to be big, like a zillion tiny space capsules about to be launched. Fearing a temporary loss of control, I pulled the car to the curb and rolled down the driver's side window. The action started quickly: one, two, three, four . . .

Some people's sneezes are so soft they are barely audible; others are backed with vocalization so loud that it causes the birds to scatter. (There is no connection between the vocal cords and the sneeze mechanism, a teacher once explained while writing a detention slip.)

Sneezes five through nine, as well as all the others to follow, were firm but not unnecessarily amplified. "Ten," in all cultures is an important number— the gateway to double digits—the basis of the decimal system. That milestone was passed quickly on the way to another significant number, "fifteen."

In some Latin Countries, the tradition of *quinceañera* is celebrated when a girl reaches that age. In the town of San Pedro on Ambergris Caye in Belize, I once saw a *quinceañera* party celebrated on the town basketball court, which was also the tennis court and party place. On an island in which even the mayor walked around barefoot, the honoree was about the only one who was shod.

If sneezes were years, I reached the legal voting age at number eighteen.

By then my situation became less of a malady and more of a challenge. No one keeps track of such things but certainly I must be approaching a record, especially when I issued my twentieth sneeze. Number ten seemed so long ago.

By then I could feel my eyes being less itchy and the pressure within dissolving. Still, there was enough ammunition inside for what would be, and still is, my personal best—twenty-one. If sneezes were indeed years, mine would now be an adult.

I am not sure what brought on such an outburst. I have never again had an experience anywhere near the number. Because I was alone, there was no response of "God bless you," following each eruption. That could have been someone else's personal best.

For the moment, the day was quiet again, and that in itself is the very best.